W9-AAX-407

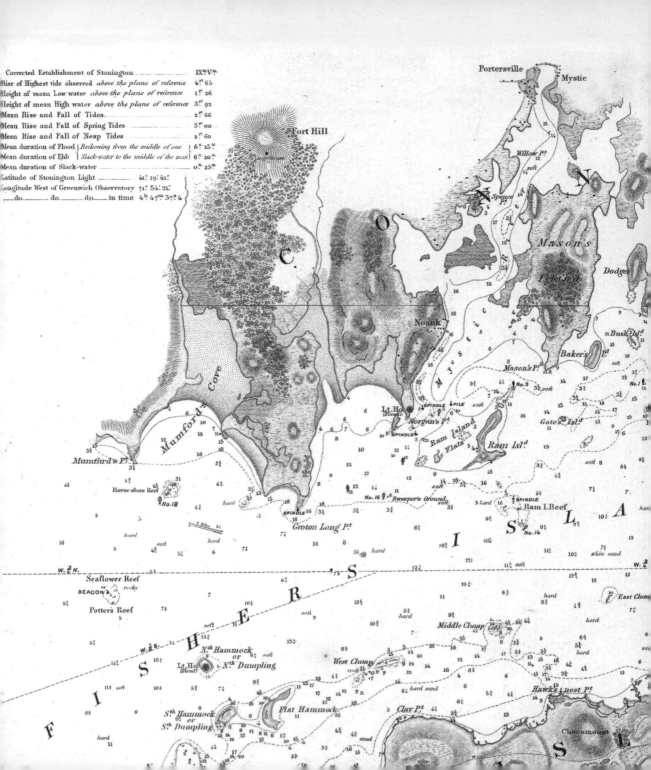

Corrected Establishment of Stonington	IX.ʰ·V.ᵐ.
Rise of Highest tide observed *above the plane of reference*	4.ᶠ·65
Height of mean Low water *above the plane of reference*	1.ᶠ·26
Height of mean High water *above the plane of reference*	3.ᶠ·92
Mean Rise and Fall of Tides.	2.ᶠ·66
Mean Rise and Fall of Spring Tides	3.ᶠ·00
Mean Rise and Fall of Neap Tides	2.ᶠ·60
Mean duration of Flood ⎰ *Reckoning from the middle of one*	6.ʰ·15.ᵐ.
Mean duration of Ebb ⎱ *Slack-water to the middle of the next*	6.ʰ·10.ᵐ.
Mean duration of Slack-water	0.ʰ·25.ᵐ.
Latitude of Stonington Light	41.º·19.′·41.″
Longitude West of Greenwich Observatory	71.º·54.′·21.″
do. do. do. in time	4.ʰ·47.ᵐ·37.ˢ·4

Fort Hill

Portersville

Mystic

C O N N

Willow P.ᵗ

soft

Spence P.ᵗ

Mason's

Island

Dodges

Noank

Mumford's
Cove

n.Bush.Isl.ᵈ

Baker's I.ᵈ

Mason's P.ᵗ

Mystic

Lt. Ho.
(Fixed)

SPINDLE

PILE

soft

Morgan's P.ᵗ

SPINDLE

Gate's Isl.ᵈ

Ram Island
Flats

Ram Isl.ᵈ

Mumford's P.ᵗ

Horse-shoe Reef

No.18

SPINDLE

Groton Long P.ᵗ

No.16

Sweeper's Ground
soft

soft

SPINDLE

Ram I.Reef

No.14

W. ¾ N.

white sand

Seaflower Reef

BEACON

rocky

East Clum

Potter's Reef

F I S H E R'S   I S L A

Middle Clump

hard

West Clump
rocky

Hawk's nest P.ᵗ

N.ᵗʰ Hammock
or
N.ᵗʰ Dumpling

Lt. Ho.
(Fixed)

Clay P.ᵗ

S.ᵗʰ Hammock
or
S.ᵗʰ Dumpling

Flat Hammock.

hard sand

Chocomount

hard

mud

S I

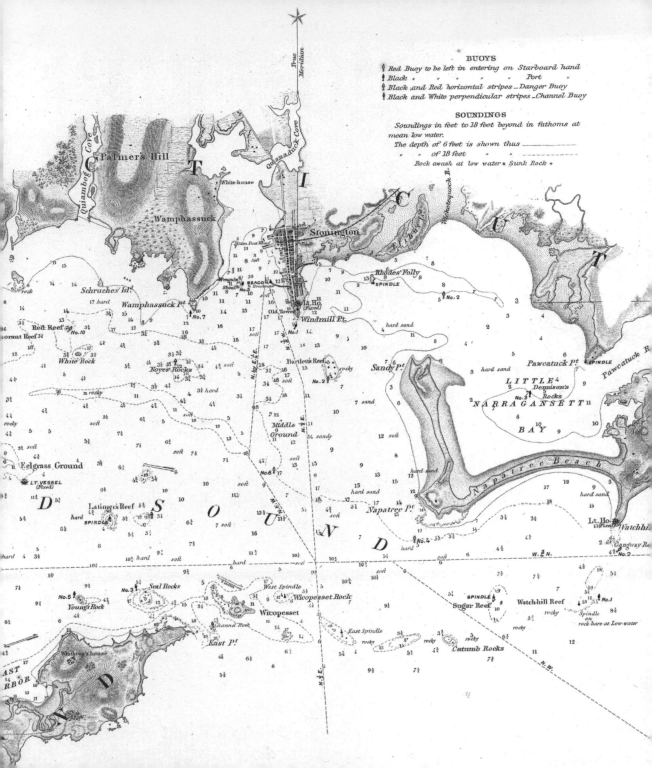

Stonington's
Old Lighthouse
and Its Keepers
1840-2013

Old Lighthouse Museum in the sharp shadows of summer in the twentieth century. *(Photo by Rollie McKenna)*

Stonington's Old Lighthouse and Its Keepers 1840-2013

by James Boylan and Betsy Wade

THE STONINGTON HISTORICAL SOCIETY
STONINGTON, CONNECTICUT

The Stonington Historical Society, Inc.
P.O. Box 103, Stonington, CT 06378

Copyright 2013 The Stonington Historical Society

Library of Congress Cataloging-in-Publication Data
Boylan, James R.
Stonington's old lighthouse and its keepers, 1840-2013
by James Boylan and Betsy Wade.
pages cm
Includes bibliographical references.
ISBN 978-0-9794013-9-8 (alk. paper)
1. Lighthouses – Connecticut – Stonington – History. 2. Lighthouse
keepers – Connecticut – Stonington – Biography. 3. Old Lighthouse
Museum (Stonington, Conn.) – History. 4. Stonington (Conn.) –
Biography. I. Wade, Betsy. II. Title.
VK1024.C8B68 2013
387.1'55097465 – dc23
2013016732

Designed by Marie A. Carija

ISBN 978-0-9794013-9-8

Gravestone in Stonington cemetery of Captain William Potter (died 1842) and Patty Barker Potter (died 1869). *(Photograph by authors)*

To the memory of
the first Keepers:
Captain William Potter
and Patty Barker Potter

Contents

INTRODUCTION

The old lighthouse sits solidly on its skirt of grass above Stonington Point, the easternmost tongue of coastline in Connecticut. It has been there now for more than 170 years, a survivor of a half-forgotten era of lighthouse construction and lighthouse keeping. Now housing the Stonington Historical Society's museum of curiosities, the building had an unquiet, even turbulent, history before outliving its original purpose and falling into another role: a place regarded with quiet affection — attracting visitors and neighbors, lighthouse buffs, picnickers, couples in love, dogwalkers, and half of the year, people looking for a place to find some history, some romance, some aura of the days of a seafaring life.

Much of its history as a working lighthouse has been buried in archives and shaky memories. Research now tells us that its initial construction produced a near-scandal; that this small place was briefly the nexus of a national conflict over control of the lighthouse establishment; that the family that first tended it paid a heavy price in ill health and poverty; that their successors fared little better. Ultimately, the record shows, American lighthouses were placed under professional administration and our lighthouse, replaced by beacons needing less intense human management, was transformed into a museum, first of its kind in the United States. This history has been murky for many years; it is now available to enrich our understanding of our rubblestone building, with its peculiar construction details.

This book shows the durability of people's regard for the Lighthouse. The pictorial material here, old and new, paintings, sketches, blueprints, photographs, woodcuts, postcards and architectural diagrams, testify to an interest that has not faded through generations. This history is occasionally obscure, sometimes grim, a story of hard times, scoundrels, cover-ups, reformers, and a good deal of rudderless drifting. It also includes the varied keepers of the lighthouse and its museum, some generous and determined people, who were enough, sometimes just barely, to bring the Lighthouse through to today.

It is time once again to study, repair, and strengthen our 1840 treasure and to assure access to it for further generations. We offer this book to preserve its history along with its fabric so future visitors can know that children have been tramping up the tower steps for one hundred and seventy — plus how many? — years.

James Boylan and Betsy Wade
August 2013

Stonington's Old Lighthouse and Its Keepers 1840-2013

Over a span of more than eight decades, many thousands have visited the Old Lighthouse Museum in Stonington. A rectangular stone structure with a curiously medieval-looking castellated tower at its front, it stands on a grassy tract just north of Stonington Point, the southern extremity of the Borough of Stonington, in the southeast corner of Connecticut. From the tower, visitors view a dramatic seascape — southeastward past Watch Hill, Rhode Island, to Block Island; south past the harbor breakwaters to a reef-filled exit to the ocean; south to distant Montauk, at the end of Long Island; and south and west to Fishers Island, an outlying fragment of New York State. Inside, the museum displays relics of war and the sea, portraits from the eighteenth and nineteenth centuries, and historical miscellany presented over decades to the museum's owner, the Stonington Historical Society.

It has been more than 120 years since the building was a working lighthouse. Like every other lighthouse constructed in the United States, surviving or vanished, it has a story — why and how it was built; its place in the national effort to encourage and protect waterborne commerce; how its builders, keepers, and their families fared; and how its work came to an end. What was originally called the Stonington Harbor Lighthouse served for nearly fifty years before its lamps were doused; then it stood for nearly four decades mostly as a damp relic; and ultimately it was preserved to become a community museum, a role it has now played longer than its term as a lighthouse. Indeed, it appears to have been the first lighthouse structure to be used as a museum in the United States.[1]

The story of the Stonington lighthouse — or, rather, lighthouses, because the lighthouse that stands today had a predecessor — begins with the waters that required their presence. Stonington harbor, less than half a mile in breadth and extending inland about a mile, was far from a perfect refuge for ships. An 1884 government document stated: "Originally it was an open bay, unprotected from southerly storms and obstructed by a shoal, having at low water a depth of but 6 feet at the shoalest part. This shoal nearly filled the inner harbor, and left but a narrow channel on either side, of a depth insufficient to permit vessels of 12 feet draught to reach the upper wharves at low water."[2]

The approaches to the harbor were even worse: To enter, ships had to navigate Fishers Island Sound, a difficult, often dangerous patch of water extending a dozen or so miles from Napatree Point, the westernmost tip of Rhode Island, to the western end of Fishers Island, which lay south of Stonington, Groton, and New London. The waters outside Stonington harbor were, and are, dotted with reefs and shoals, many lurking just below low-water mark. In the age of sail and even later, accurate, careful, protected navigation was the price of safe passage. An edition of the *United States Coast Pilot* published as late as the mid-twentieth century says of Fishers Island Sound that "the entire area is exceedingly treacherous, being characterized by boulder patches which rise abruptly from deeper water."[3]

Stonington's harbor came to life around 1750, roughly a hundred years after the English first settled the area. A village grew on the eastern shore, which offered the harbor's deeper water, and spread across the narrow point to the shore of Little Narragansett Bay on the east. The inhabitants were primarily fishing families, but before the end of the eighteenth century Stonington-Port, as the settlement came to be called, had become a base for coastal trade and voyages to distant seas. Commercial activity in Stonington was recognized as early as 1790 in an act of Congress, which designated it a "port of delivery" —

Facing page: Fisher's Island Sound, shown on the 1877 United States Coast Survey. Through Stonington Point, also called Windmill Point, runs a line marked "True Meridian." The chart designates both an "Old Tower" and "Lt. Ho. Fixed." (*Authors' collection*)

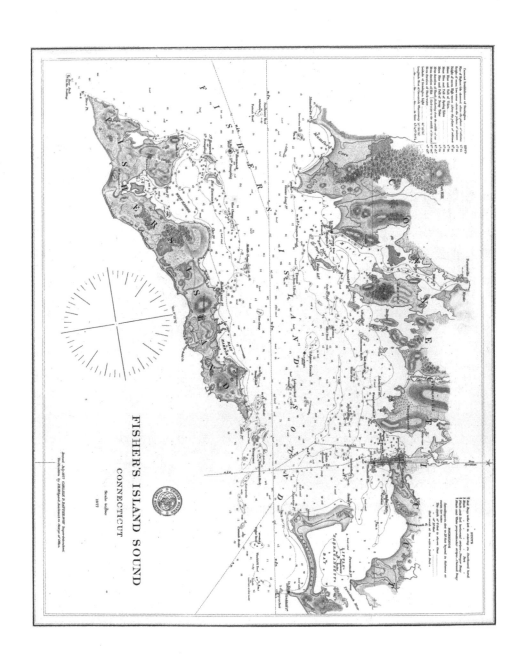

FISHER'S ISLAND SOUND
CONNECTICUT
Scale 1:40000
1877

that is, a place where goods could be landed — with an appointed "surveyor" of customs, as differentiated from the higher-ranking "collector" of customs.[4]

Until the start of the nineteenth century, the only aids to navigation in the approaches to Stonington harbor were improvised markers, often privately placed spindles. In 1800 Dr. William Lord of Stonington-Port announced in the area's newspapers that, having raised funds, he had "erected an iron spear about 13 feet long, with a large black ball and white vane on top, upon the rock of Latimer in Fisher's Island Sound." *The American Coast Pilot*, the most widely used guide to American waters, advised skippers to avoid Fishers Island Sound and Stonington altogether by passing outside of Fishers Island. There were no instructions for entering Stonington harbor.[5]

The village, which was incorporated in 1801 as the Borough of Stonington,

A closeup from the transfer print on a Liverpool jug depicting the Battle of Stonington, August 1814. The jug was manufactured before 1820 and the picture was probably based on an oral account of the battle. This tiny section shows a flag flying behind a cannon, and farther toward the Point a structure with a pyramid roof and a knob or spire on top, evidently a beacon. No historical account of the battle mentions such an aid to navigation.

a subsection of the Town of Stonington, was already developing a distinct and vigorous identity. The little seaport twice repelled British attacks — the first a brief foraging raid by *HMS Rose* at the start of the American Revolution; the second, during the War of 1812, a prolonged bombardment by a Royal Navy squadron under the famed Captain Thomas Hardy in August 1814, stoutly resisted by Stonington cannons and militia. The only near-contemporary depiction of the battle, a drawing on a Liverpool jug created before 1820, appears to show a primitive aid to navigation — a pyramid-roofed structure with a spire on top, at the extreme southern tip of Stonington Point. However, there is no known written record of such a beacon. The second encounter came to be known as the Battle of Stonington.

An 1819 gazetteer offered this appraisal: "The maritime situation and interests of the town have given a direction to the pursuits and habits of its citizens; and Stonington has become conspicuous as a nursery of seamen, distinguished for their enterprise, perseverance and courage." Even as these words were published, a young Stonington skipper, Nathaniel Brown Palmer, was in the Southern Ocean, on his way to becoming an early discoverer of Antarctica.[6]

The commercial waterfront centered on a district lying along the harbor west of present-day Cannon Square. As early as 1819, Stonington berthed ten to fifteen fishing vessels, three packets on regular trips to New York, coasting vessels hauling fish, cheese, grain, and other local produce, and a pilot boat to guide vessels into the harbor. Responding to a local petition, an Army engineer on "topographical" service noted the extreme vulnerability of the harbor to winds off the ocean from the south-southeast and recommended construction of a breakwater. Between 1828 and 1831 the federal government underwrote such a breakwater — constructed by the Stonington builder Charles Hewitt Smith — extending west from the harbor shore, with a flat crown and bollards that permitted its use as a loading dock.[7]

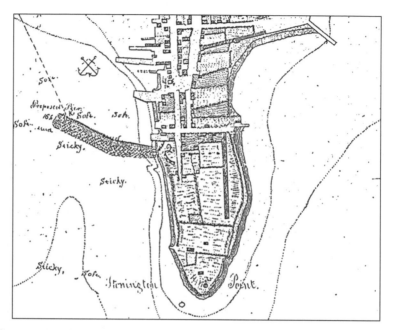

The ornamental inscription on the face of this map says: "The Harbour and Borough of Stonington/ County of New-London/ State of Connecticut/ Surveyed and Drawn by Lieut. J. Prescott, 1st rgt of art/ Septb 1827/Eng dept U. States Top Bureau." Uncoded, the abbreviations say the artist was in the first regiment of artillery in the engineering department of the topographical bureau. The planned breakwater extends westward from the shore. The round shape at the tip is inscribed "light."

The first breakwater extending west from the old Atwood factory, now Stonington Commons. It appears here as it was before the 1938 hurricane tossed the flat-topped stonework around and tore up the bollards.

The First Lighthouse

After 1820, Stonington became a candidate for a lighthouse. To do so, it had to gain the attention of the federal legislators and bureaucracy that financed and built lighthouses. From its inception in 1789, the federal government recognized the need to protect seagoing commerce. One of the earliest acts of the First United States Congress was to assume responsibility for lighthouses and other aids to navigation by adopting "An Act for the Establishment and Support of Lighthouses, Beacons, Buoys, and Public Piers." It provided for the transfer of all existing lighthouses to federal authority and for federally financed repair and maintenance. In addition, it set a precedent for constructing more lighthouses.[8]

The first lighthouse built entirely with federal funds was completed at Montauk Point, across from Stonington on Long Island, in 1797. There were already colonial-era beacons to the east and west of Stonington. One, in New London harbor, dating from before 1760, was replaced by the federal government in 1801. To the east, the government eventually responded to fifteen years of petitions from Stonington and nearby Westerly and in 1807 built a light at Watch Hill, Rhode Island, to replace a beacon dating from 1745.[9]

In the thirty-odd years after passage of the act governing lighthousess, control of their siting, construction, buildings, maintenance, and supply was under control of the Treasury Department, which shifted the responsibility within the department until it landed on the desk of Stephen Pleasonton, a bureaucrat with a modest title, Fifth Auditor. Pleasonton had no particular maritime expertise, but was politically well connected, in part because he had saved important national documents when the British burned Washington in the War of 1812. Moreover, he was an all-but-perfect bureaucrat, skillful at paperwork, adroit at shifting blame, and, it proved, adept at survival.

This illustration, evidently made from Wamphassuc Point, is titled "West View of the Borough of Stonington." It shows church towers and masts and, at the Point, to the far right, a light tower for navigation, probably the first lighthouse. The engraving is copied from John Warner Barber's *Connecticut Historical Collections* (1836).

Pleasonton inherited as his chief partner Winslow Lewis, a retired sea captain from Boston who had taken out a patent on a parabolic reflector light, designed to project a beam into the dark. Lewis claimed to have invented it, but in fact he had merely adapted the Argand light already widely used in Europe. The federal government bought the patent from him in 1812 and granted him a virtual monopoly in equipping the nation's lighthouses, which he maintained for many years. A 21st-century article about Lewis's career identified him as a "scalawag."[10]

The Fifth Auditor's era, which lasted more than three decades, became notorious for its slipshod methods and resistance to change. The lighthouse construction system as it developed called for local collectors of customs — in Stonington's case, the collector based in nearby New London — to obtain bids for construction of lighthouses, invariably to accept the lowest, and to exercise such supervision as they wished over execution. Not surprisingly, the result was frequently shoddy, unstable workmanship, combined with badly installed, ill-maintained, and malfunctioning lights. Moreover, Pleasonton and Lewis were instrumental in delaying the introduction of the superior Fresnel lamps from France, which were available as early as the 1820s. More than 250 lighthouses were constructed under Pleasonton's authority, but many did not outlast his tenure.

Pleasonton's attention turned to Stonington in 1822 when Congress, authorizing a package of lighthouses on the East Coast, appropriated $3,500 to build a lighthouse on what was then commonly called Windmill Point, at the lower end of Stonington Borough. The government acquired half an acre at the tip of the Point for $300 from two owners, Otis Pendleton and S. F. Denison, in May 1823. Responsibility for carrying out the project then fell to the new collector of customs at New London, Richard Law, who advertised the specifications in local newspapers in June 1823.[11]

The plan, as published, called for a stone lighthouse tower thirty feet tall (the standard height for a harbor entrance), resting on a deep foundation and capped with a glass dome containing the lantern, with a vent to release the smoke from the whale oil that fueled the lights. The adjacent dwelling house

This portrait of Captain Thomas Burtch, painted about 1835, is attributed to Orlando Hand Bears of Sag Harbor, Long Island. It has long been in the Old Lighthouse Museum. *(Photographs by Mary Beth Baker)*

The distant background of the Burtch portrait contains an image of what is probably the original lighthouse on Stonington Point.

for the keeper was to be built of stone, one story high, 680 square feet, divided into two rooms, each with a closet. Nothing was said about furnishings or other domestic equipment. There was also a cellar. A well was to be dug at a convenient distance. Finally, the plan specified that the lights themselves were to be fitted up by Pleasonton's ally Winslow Lewis.

No architectural drawing of the first lighthouse has been found. There is a hint of its design in a Pleasonton letter that says that the Stonington specifications should be like those for the Old Field Point lighthouse, on the north shore of Long Island. The original tower at Old Field Point is long gone, but the keeper's house, built in 1824, survives, and suggests that the dwelling might at best be called "cozy." The Stonington site is marked on an 1827 map of the Borough, and the placement of the tower and the keeper's dwelling are indicated in a later sketch by John Bishop of New London. The tower also appears in the distance in the widely reproduced 1836 drawing of the Borough by John Barber and in the background of a painting of Captain Thomas Burtch now hanging in the Old Lighthouse Museum.[12]

By July 21, 1823, nine bids had been received and Benjamin Chace of Newport, who came in at $2,500, $70 lower than any local bidder, was awarded the work. The project was to be completed by November 20, 1823 — less than four months. It got done, and $583 of the appropriation of $3,500 was returned to the Treasury.[13]

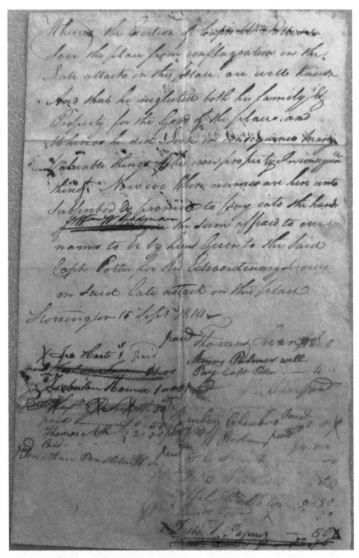

Just after the Battle of Stonington in 1814, comrades of Captain William Potter took up a public collection seeking to assist him in recovering from his war losses.

Finding a Keeper

In the meantime, the collector needed to search for Stonington's first lighthouse keeper. Even before the contract was awarded, Stonington Borough selected its hometown favorite — William Potter, who had served as captain of the Eighth Company, Thirtieth Regiment, of Connecticut Militia during the War of 1812, most notably during the Battle of Stonington, in which, from all accounts, he had performed heroically. Immediately after the battle, the members of his company took up a collection:

> Whereas the exertion of Capt. Wm Potter to save the place from conflagration in the late attack on this place are well known and that he neglected both his family & Property for the good of the place and whereas he did loose in consequence many valuable things of his own property in consequence thereof now we whose names are here unto subscribed do promise to pay . . . the sum affixed to our names to be given to him.

Potter served as captain until May 15, 1815, a few months after the end of the war, when he was honorably discharged by his commanding officer, Major General William Williams, himself a native of Stonington, and was directed to supervise the election of a successor, which he did.[14]

What else is known about William Potter? Family records state that he was born in London, England, on February 9, 1778. In the War of 1812, he was charged, as a captain of militia, with escorting fourteen deserters from the Royal Navy frigate *Acasta* who had been welcomed in Stonington to New London. Edmund Fanning, Stonington's famed circumnavigator, recalled in his letter of recommendation that Potter was a confidential courier between Fanning and the American naval hero Stephen Decatur, whose squadron was trapped by the

Royal Navy in the Thames River north of New London. An account from Stonington of the great storm of September 1815 mentioned the destruction of a rope walk operated by a "Mr. Potter." [15]

There was also a large family. According to family records, by about 1802 Potter was married to Martha Barker of Norwich, who used the name Patty. By 1823, William and Patty had had ten children, of whom eight — ranging in age from seventeen to less than a year — were still living, destined to share the 680 square feet of the keeper's house with their parents. One of the letters of recommendation referred to the family's "indigent circumstances." Clearly, Captain Potter needed the job. [16]

In support of Potter, the Borough went straight to the top — to President Monroe, who had visited Stonington early in his first term and had met the veterans of 1814. The petition read:

> To His Excellency James Monroe
> President of the United States
> We the subscribed inhabitants of Stonington and others beg leave to recommend to your favourable Notice Capt. William Potter of Stonington [words missing] estimable and meritorious candidate for Keeper of the Light House at Stonington Point.
>
> With deference we would submit a few considerations with reference to his claims upon the good opinion of the President — he has a family of [6] Daughters and 2 Sons: During the late war he commanded the Stonington Borough Militia; underwent innumerable privations and hardships & principally thro his instrumentality & exertions the Boro, was saved from conflagration during the Bombardment of A.D. 1814.
>
> In addition to which his daily labour & industry afford but a precarious and scanty subsistence, for a growing family —
>
> His fidelity and ability are the surest guarantee for a prompt Discharge of his Duties — We think his appointment would meet the public approbation & serve the public interest and relieve a meritorious Citizen.

Facing page: Comrades-at-arms and friends sent a petition, of which this is part, to President Monroe to support William Potter for the new post of lighthouse keeper in Stonington. It was dated April 22, 1822, and included 90 signatures. *(Photographed by the authors at the National Archives, Washington)*

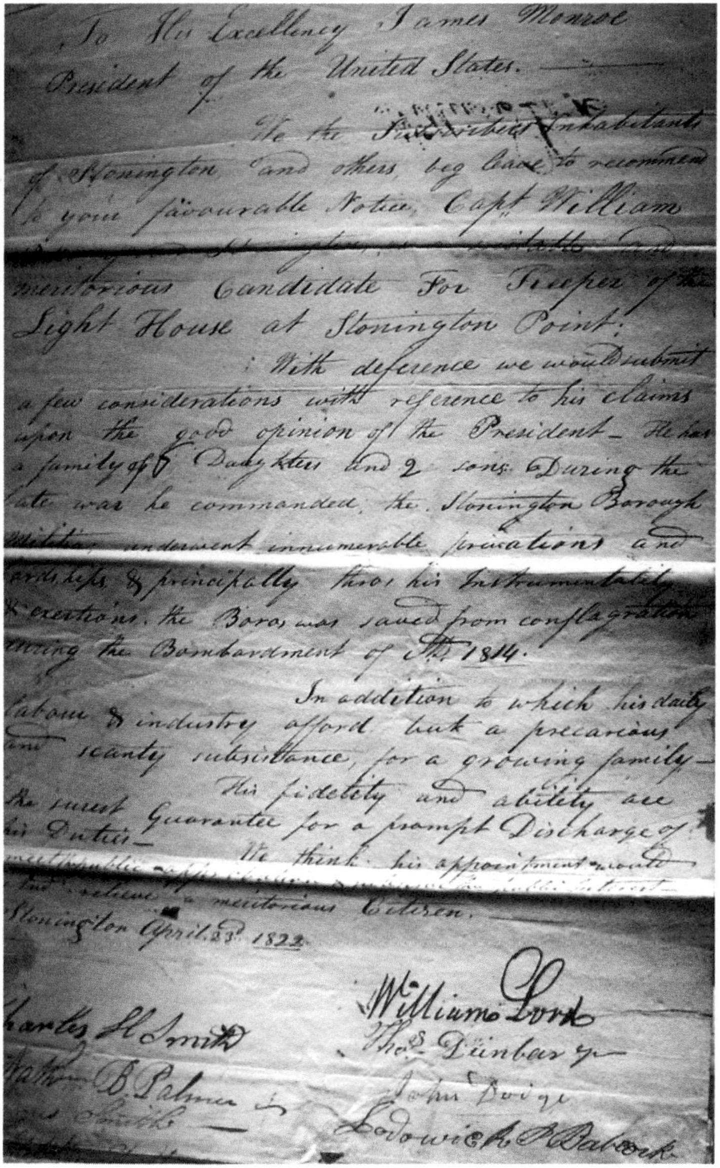

Appended to the petition, on three sheets of paper, were the signatures of no fewer than ninety friends and neighbors, including some who had served under him.[17]

Other recommendations arrived as the lighthouse was built, none more noteworthy than that from Captain Fanning, addressed to Commodore Isaac Chauncey, a commander on Lake Ontario during the War of 1812 and now a member of the Navy's governing board:

> My dear Sir. I take the liberty to address this to You in the cause and aid of sterling merit. Will you have the goodness to call on the Hon Secretary of the Treasury and on Mr. S. Pleasonton, 5th auditor and use your friendly aid to obtain the appointment of Capt. William Potter to the tending of the Light House now erecting at this place?
>
> Capt. Potter is a worthy citizen, has a large family of small children in indigent circumstances, is a real friend to his country, he commanded the company of Militia of this Borough at the time of the attack on it by Commodore Hardy, and his behaviour & conduct on that occasion is beyond praise and was one of the few confidential persons employed by me during the war in traveling night & day to convey my observations of the movements of the Enemy's squadron to our deceased and much lamented friend, Commodore Decatur.
>
> And well knowing your warm and & honourable feelings towards true merit, I do not hesitate to request your friendly aid on this particular occasion.
>
> And am with sentiments of the highest Respect & Esteem your sincere friend & Obt. Servt., Edmund Fanning [18]

The collector in New London, Richard Law, was obligated to make a recommendation to Pleasonton. In his letter, he ignored the broad local support for Potter and discussed two applicants without leaning to one or the other. Potter's rival was Joshua Sanford, a ship's master retired because of age (he was in his sixties) and infirmity. A pair of supporters signing a letter for him said he deserved help as a "fellow Mason." Law described Sanford as "very reputable Ship master in New York," who had returned to his native Stonington, where he was supporting his aged parents and an "Idiot Brother." Of Captain Potter, Law said nothing specific, not even mentioning his war service, but said of both candidates that "either would give satisfaction in the execution of their duty to the Government as well as the Commercial interests of the country." He added: "They are both Republicans and strenuous supporters of the Administration of the Country."[19]

Pleasonton forwarded a recommendation for Potter to the White House, and Potter was appointed by President Monroe on October 25, 1823. He was sworn in by the collector on December 29, and signed an elaborate oath of office:

> I, William Potter of Stonington in the State of Connecticut having been appointed Keeper of the Light House at Stonington Point do solemnly sincerely and truly swear, that I will diligently and faithfully execute the duties of said office of Light House Keeper and will use the best of my endeavors to prevent and detect frauds in relation to the duties imposed by the Laws of the United States and I further swear that I will support the Constitution of the United States.   Wm Potter [20]

On the next day, December 30, Collector Law's notice in New London's *Connecticut Gazette* announced: "A Light-House has been erected on Stonington Point and is lighted up from the sitting to the rising of the Sun." It provided bearings for the light from points in the vicinity, such as the Watch Hill Light and Latimer's Reef. [21]

Captain Potter undertook his duties with the new year; he was destined to serve until his death, looking out across the waters where he had once seen a Royal Navy squadron arrayed.

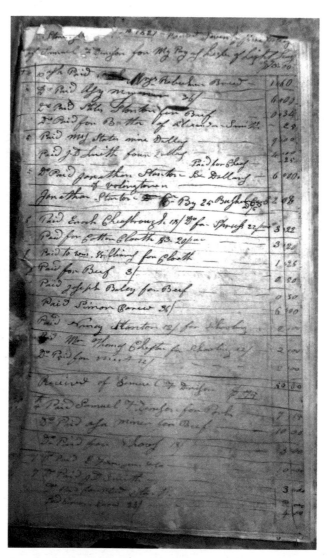

A page of Potter's personal account book for 1827 shows purchases of necessities such as beef and butter to feed the family.

Washout?

What were the obligations of Captain Potter's new job? Keeping the light burning, of course. But in that era keepers had to find their own way. When Pleasonton finally issued a set of instructions in 1835, they no doubt reflected what most keepers, including Potter, had already learned. They were to record the amount oil consumed each night. The lamps had to be kept scrupulously clean, and the wicks trimmed. No unexcused absences, of course. As to personal conduct: "You are not to sell, or permit to be sold, any spirituous liquors on the premises of the United States; but will treat with civility and attention, such strangers as may visit the Light-house under your charge, and as may conduct themselves in an orderly manner." Potter's earliest account and log book, 1824 to 1828, survives in local Stonington records. It reveals no notable events in that period, beyond the crash of a sea bird into a lighthouse pane. There were regular deliveries of whale oil and other necessities by Winslow Lewis, holder of the monopoly.[22]

It soon became apparent that all was not well with the lighthouse. Placed too close to the shore and unshielded, it deteriorated on the inside and was threatened by the waters at its threshold. At the start of 1831, the keeper reported: "A gail of wind on [January 15] washed off twelve feet of the Bank South of the Lighthouse which leaves But twenty feet from the light house to the edge of the Bank which is wearing a way fast."[23]

That May, a new collector, W. Ingoldsby Crawford, visited the lighthouse and observed to Pleasonton:

I have found that both the Light House and the keepers dwelling house at Stonington point evidently need considerable repair. They were not well built originally. The mortar contained too great a proportion of sand; it was wet up with seawater, in a cold season of the year, and exposed immediately to the action of frost. In every storm of rain the water penetrates the buildings, damages their floors and furniture, interrupts the ordinary vocations, and imminently exposes the health of the keeper's family. It is believed that a substantial coat of Roman cement [cement impervious to water when set], put on in the month of July or August, would effectually remedy the evil. The expense would probably amount to one hundred and fifty or two hundred dollars. [24]

More than eight months later, Crawford again checked in with Pleasonton, telling a story of inaction by then all too customary in the lighthouse establishment:

In pursuance of your instructions of May 31st I made a contract for plastering the light house at Stonington point with Roman cement, to be completed, under the supervision of the keeper, by the first of September. The contractor failed of performance within the time stipulated. . . . The house was very imperfectly built at first, and no degree of repair can ever make it good. The outer walls have so long been penetrated by every wind and rain, that the timbers and floors within are decayed and rotten; they must be renewed, or the house must be abandoned. The location of it, in my opinion, was as injudicious, as the construction was defective. . . . Unless some barrier be erected against further encroachments, it is probable that the house, in the course of two or three years more, will be swept away.

That spring, a full year after he raised the subject, Crawford sent to Pleasonton an estimate for building a protective sea wall. Nothing happened, beyond money for minor repairs.[25]

Such troubles, and others even more serious at other lighthouses built by Pleasonton and company, were so widespread that eventually they burst into public view. Among the instigators were the brothers Edmund and George W. Blunt, who had inherited *The Atlantic Coast Pilot* from their father. In two long

Facing page: Potter's working account book survives, but the record indicates that the labor was monotonous save for a bird that flew into a pane in the Lighthouse lantern.

Jan			
1			
2			
3			
4			
5			
6			
7			Tube glasses B. 1
8			
9			
10			
11			
12			
13			
14			
15			Tube glasses B 1
16			
17			
18			
19			
20			
21			
22			One Pane glass
23			Broken by foul
24			
25			
26			
27			
28			

Potter's official log for the first quarter of 1831 records that the sea had come within twenty feet of the Lighthouse. *(Photographed by the authors at the National Archives, Waltham)*

letters to the secretary of the treasury, they declared, based on complaints from shipmasters, that the lighthouse system was badly managed, that it was inferior technically to the systems of Britain and France, and that its deficiencies represented a continuing danger to sea traffic.[26]

Their indictment was taken up by Senator John Davis of Massachusetts and the Senate Committee on Commerce, and in March 1837 Congress put a halt to all lighthouse construction projected in current legislation until each project was examined by a naval officer. The result was the stoppage of work on thirty-one proposed lighthouses. A year later, Congress ordered an inspection by Navy officers of existing lighthouses as well.[27]

This legislation brought young Lieutenant George M. Bache (who some years later died tragically in a storm while commanding a Coastal Survey vessel) to Stonington in 1838. He reported that he found the structures and the lights in good enough order, the wooden stairway in the tower having just been replaced. But he added:

> The point of land on which the buildings stand is much exposed to the action of the waters, during heavy south and southwesterly gales. High water mark now lies within 45 feet of the tower, and the earth has been washed away to within 30 feet of the base. According to the account of the light keeper, 22 feet of the bank has been carried away from the extremity of the point since 1823, and the same action has been going on, though in less degree, to the eastward and westward of the dwelling. It will be advisable to protect these buildings from the further encroachment of the sea by constructing a wall.[28]

Pleasonton shrugged off this and much more severe criticisms — for example, Bache's finding that the revolving light at Watch Hill did not revolve at all and could be mistaken for the stationary Stonington light. Bache also found the light at Morgan's Point almost too dim to be seen. And so it was, up and down the coast. Yet Pleasonton survived the crisis.[29]

A Second Lighthouse

Toward the end of 1839, the then New London collector, Charles F. Lester, asked John Bishop, a New London builder, to draw a plan for a protective seawall at Stonington Point, as recommended by Lieutenant Bache. Lester submitted the drawing and a cost estimate of $12,000 to Pleasonton. Pleasonton blanched; he declared that the seawall plan was "so extravagant I did not think to lay it before Congress." In addition, he may have thought that such a request might call attention to his bad judgment in building the lighthouse on such a vulnerable site in the first place.[30]

Instead, Pleasonton deputized I.W.P. Lewis, a nephew of Winslow Lewis, who was a civil engineer and a budding lighthouse designer, to inspect the ground and plan a second lighthouse. In April 1840, Pleasonton reported to the collector:

> Mr. Lewis informs me that there is a lot of land for sale near the Lighthouse at Stonington, which would answer perfectly well for a Lighthouse, and that the buildings might be put upon it for the same sum which a wall around the present buildings would cost. I am therefore decidedly in favor of purchasing a sufficient quantity of the lot, and of removing the present buildings to it. The old lot could probably be sold for something afterwards.[31]

At this point, apparently, Pleasonton did not have in mind a new lighthouse but a full-scale transplant of the original lighthouse and keeper's dwelling. He wrote to Lester on May 5, 1840:

> On securing a good title to the Lot, you will advertise for proposals to remove both the Light House and Keeper's house to the best protection

on the new lot. If a new Lantern or lamps should be required, it will be necessary to make provision for them in the advertisement. The lantern should be made however according to an improved plan to contain large plate glass, of which Mr. I. W. P. Lewis, at Boston, can give you a description.[32]

By the time Pleasonton wrote again to Collector Lester on June 4, 1840, a plan for a new lighthouse had emerged, specifying a structure with "dwelling and light house united":

The plan of the new building appears to be a suitable one, and you

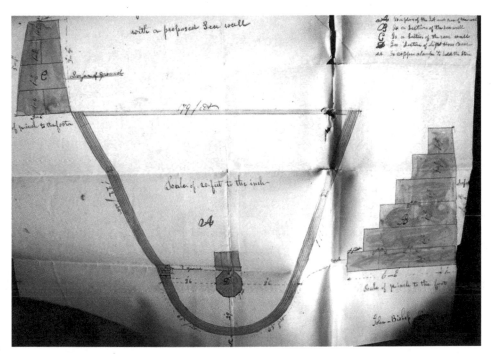

Diagram of the siting of a potential seawall to protect the first lighthouse from being "swept away" by the encroaching tides. Stephen Pleasonton, in Washington, considered this option too expensive. *(Photographed by the authors at the National Archives, Washington)*

will advertise for proposals to erect the buildings, the contractor using the old materials as far as they may be found suitable. For the lantern, lamps and reflectors, you will contract with Mr. Lewis, so that they are not to be embraced by the contract for the building. You will appoint a suitable mechanic to oversee the work and will give him particular instructions to attend daily whilst it is in progress and see that it is faithfully done. You may allow him not exceeding 2 50/100 dollars [$2.50] per day.[33]

The government's acquisition, 1.5 acres, lay a hundred yards or less to the north and east of the 1823 lighthouse, on substantially higher ground and beyond the reach of the sea, but still overlooking the approaches to the harbor. The sellers of the plot were James and Lucretia Morris and Peter Crary, who operated the grist mill at Wind Mill Point. The price of the land was $3,600.[34]

On June 23, 1840, the collector, Charles F. Lester, in his role as "Superintendent of Lighthouses east of New Haven on the coast of the United States," signed a contract with John Bishop of New London, creator of the discarded seawall proposal. The work was to be completed by September 30, a few days more than three months from the date of the contract. Until the new light was ready, Bishop was to provide "a temporary tower & Lantern that the light may be exhibited as usual, making use of the present lighting apparatus for the purpose." Rather than create a temporary tower, it appears, Bishop left the old tower standing at the Point; indeed, according to later maps and drawings it is evident that despite all the fears that it would be swept into the sea it stood for years, even decades, afterward.[35]

In addition, the use to be made of materials from the old lighthouse and keeper's house was suggested but not specified in the contract:

It is also further understood and agreed that s[ai]d Bishop may have the old Light House or Keeper's present dwelling as they now are or tear them down in order to use such of the materials as will answer this contract in the erection of the New buildings, but if he commences taking either of them to pieces he is bound to take the same entirely down and throw the useless materials upon the adjoining beach for the purpose of a breakwater.

There is no way to ascertain whether stone from the older structures was incorporated in the new, as is often assumed, or whether the leavings — probably

Cistern and well were placed near the south wall of the new lighthouse. They provided access to fresh water without requiring a trip outdoors. Today's visitors sometimes hesitate to walk across the modern glass covering because of the cavern below. *(Photograph by authors.)*

This lamp, which used inside reflectors, was designed by Winslow Lewis and a colleague, Benjamin Hemmenway, in 1844. It was the standard lamp in lighthouses until the end of the Winslow Lewis era in 1852, when the more advanced Fresnel lenses began to appear. *(Photograph from the U.S. Lighthouse Society, courtesy of the Smithsonian Institution)*

the stones from the keeper's house — ended up as rip-rap at the point.

The contract went on with more than 2,200 words of specifications for the structure itself: the area and depth of the cellar, the dimensions and thickness of the walls, the type of mortar to be used, the dimensions of the rooms and the doors, the shape and size of the tower, the placement of a well and a cistern, the size and placement of the outdoor privy, and, most specifically, "a cooking stove called 'The Improved Yankee' made by Gardner Chilson & Co. of Boston." The curiously medieval motifs of the structure were specified as well:

> On top of the double walls (on the front & two ends of the house) to be laid a blocking course one foot thick & projecting over one foot — This blocking course to be surmounted by battlements placed at equal spaces of two feet, each battlement to be 4 feet high 2 feet wide & one foot thick . . . . Under the center of each battlement beneath the blocking course to be placed a corbel or bracket to project 8 inches to be each one foot high & . . . in the thickness of the wall — To be two openings left in the front wall of the house for windows each 4 by 4 ft. - & three feet above the level of the house floor — Each opening to have a stone cap, supported by corbels — the cap projecting 8 inches from the wall & the corbels in proportion . . .

There was also the description of the roof that was destined to cause much trouble: "The roof of the house to slope from the front wall to the rear with an inclination of one inch to the foot." That is, it was to be a virtually flat shed roof.[36]

The lighthouse specifications did not bear the name of a designer. Eventually Pleasonton blamed I.W.P. Lewis for its flaws — most notably, its ineffective roof — but the execution was attributable to the builder, Bishop, and indeed the design itself was probably his as well, given that contractors who wrote specifications for a lighthouse were almost always given the contract. No evidence has been found that Lester placed the new lighthouse out for bid, as instructed by Pleasonton, nor do the records reveal a list of competing bids, as was the case with the first Stonington lighthouse. The circumstances point to an inside deal between Lester and Bishop, both active Democrats.[37]

On September 7, 1840, Lester submitted to Washington an estimate of the cost of the project — $5,721. When the price of the land, $3,600, and the cost of the new lights was added in, the total was almost what the proposed and rejected seawall would have cost. But there were more costs ahead. A full seventeen months later, long after the work was completed, Lester filed a document stating that the contract had been completed as of October 27, 1840, and further certified that the contract's terms had been fulfilled.[38]

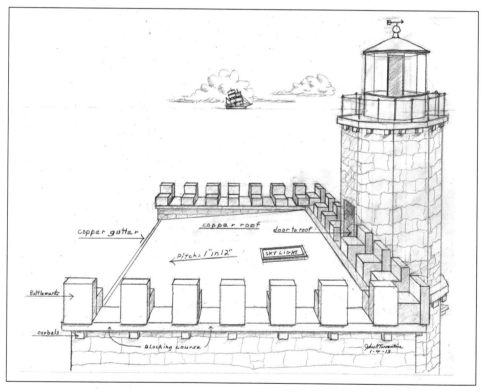

No plans for the second lighthouse survive, although there are detailed specifications for its construction. From these, the Stonington designer John H. Turrentine in 2013 drew this view looking down on the top of the building, showing its curiously medieval design. The nearly flat shed roof, barely sloping toward Little Narragansett Bay, leaked from the start.

"Shameful Built"

L ester's belated execution of these formalities was a response to his small part in a further crisis developing for the lighthouse establishment. In fact, by 1842 Lester was no longer even the collector. In January 1842, John Tyler, who had succeeded to the presidency on the death of President William Henry Harrison a few months before, began to remove holdover officeholders, among them such collectors as Lester. The new collector was Wolcott Huntington, of a famous Norwich, Connecticut, family, a descendant of the first collector at New London, General Jedidiah Huntington. [39]

The new collector proved to be vigorous and irascible. Huntington paid a call in Stonington on March 24, 1842, and hastened to report to Washington:

> Complaints of the new Light House at Stonington induced me to go over there yesterday and examine it. The roof leaks badly and was bad while it was built — the copper was not properly secured about the walls. The Keeper said they state that it had been so from the time it was built — as the contract proposals connected with the building are in your office I respectfully give this informally on my own, is that the building will require a wood roof and when it is put on should be raised so that the upper story may be used by the family, as the building is very damp and ever will be, as it was not filled out from the walls but plastered directly on the walls.[40]

By April 7, Huntington was advertising in local newspapers for bids on remodeling and repairing the roof. He specified a "barn roof," rising six inches to the foot, to replace the flat roof. Further, he said, the "battlement walls" were to be taken down and new walls to be carried up at the edges to make room in the new second floor; a flight of stairs was to be built, and windows placed at each end of the floor. High-quality materials were to be used throughout.[41]

The New London collector, Wolcott Huntington, angry that the Lighthouse leaked, required the installation of a new pitched "barn roof" rising six inches to the foot to its peak behind the tower rather than the one inch to the foot specified earlier. This allowed the keeper and family to use the second floor and to stay drier. This architectural drawing by Charles Hewitt Smith and Atwood Brayton, for repairs to the dwelling portion, is the earliest found for this building. *(Photographed in the National Archives by the authors)*

In the midst of this upheaval, William Potter died, on May 10, 1842, at the presumed age of sixty-four, cause not recorded. For more than eighteen years, he and his family had lived in the discomfort of two keeper's dwellings, while he carried out his duties, so far as is known, without pause. In the interval, the Potters' eldest surviving daughter, Esther Ann, had gone off to be married and had died. One more daughter, Caroline, had been born. With Captain Potter gone, the family comprised his widow, Patty, about 60 years old, and six offspring — a 32-year-old daughter, Eliza; William, 25 years old; Nancy, 21 years old; Fanny, about 20 years old; Dyer Barker, just turned 20; and the youngest, Caroline, about 12. Two other daughters were married and had no doubt left home.[42]

No obituaries or other tributes to Captain Potter have been found, despite his long and faithful service to his country. Stonington had no newspaper at that time, and the area's other papers took no note. Nor does the official correspondence contain any notes of recognition or sympathy. Instead, Pleasonton on May 14 sent the following note to Huntington:

> I enclose the appointment of Mrs. Potter, widow of William Potter, deceased, late Keeper, as temporary Keeper of the Stonington Lighthouse, which you will be pleased to deliver to her. Instructions are not needed, as it is presumed that the copy furnished to her late husband were left in her possession.

The appointment was in keeping with previous practice. For example, the keeper at Morgan Point, in nearby Noank, was the widow of the previous keeper. In a month, Patty Potter received her permanent appointment as her husband's successor.[43]

On May 17, 1842, Huntington signed a contract with two Stonington artisans, Charles Hewitt Smith and Atwood Brayton, to carry out the repairs and alterations. In hiring Smith and Brayton, he had in his employ Stonington's master craftsmen and masons. Smith had not only assembled the Stonington Harbor breakwater but had constructed durable lighthouses elsewhere on the East Coast. Why he was not offered the opportunity to build the lighthouse a few blocks from his home in the Borough remains attributable only to politics.

Smith and Brayton appended to their contract two drawings of the lighthouse as it was to be repaired, the earliest depiction of the 1840 lighthouse known to have survived.[44]

On June 6, Huntington wrote to Pleasonton to report that workers had removed "the copper from the roof of the dwelling at Stonington Light House. I went over & took with me two men [Smith and Brayton] to examine the building & a more shameful built building I never have seen — the mortar was poor indeed, as for cement . . . you could remove any of the stones on the inside of the walls & they were as clear of the mortar as when they were blasted...." Smith and Brayton weighed in with their first report on June 12, a roughly written compendium of shabby construction and corners cut, a litany of rotting wood, disintegrating cement — "the battlement walls . . . were laid in very poor mortar which was made of beach sand" — and cheap materials.[45]

In the meantime, Huntington became even more vehement, his handwriting so agitated that it was scarcely legible:

> There seems to be dishonesty somewhere connected with the building of the Stonington Light House, and as yet I cannot fully satisfy myself about it — Mrs Potter & her family wished me to write to you, that Mr. [I.W.P.] Lewis of Boston who was there while the building was in progress, said repeatedly that it was not according to the contracts, & that it would not answer & expected Mr. Potter to oversee the work, but Mr Lester told him [,] Mr Potter, that it was no business of Mr Lewis — nor his, and that neither of them had anything to do with it — Mr Lewis said that Mr Lester ought to be broken as superintendent and also Bishop the contractor — The Potter family all speak of Mr Lewis as a gentleman & one who seems to feel anxious that the work should be well done & they wish me to refer you to Mr Lewis for the truth of their statements.[46]

Smith and Brayton added details in a second report that Huntington appended to a letter he sent to Pleasonton on June 15. Huntington also enclosed a letter from G.R. Hallam, surveyor of the port, apparently a friend of the Potters:

> I have conversed with Mrs. Potter this morning. She says the house leaked so the first rain after they moved into it, that they were obliged to take up their carpets & dry their bedding & that every succeeding rainstorm

The regularity of the rubblestone at the second-story level, laid at the time of the repairs in 1842, contrasts with the uneven masonry below. *(Authors' photograph)*

it has leaked more or less ever since. In the course of this winter in severe weather, her daughters would frequently find their bed-covering frozen — caused by the dampness of the walls.

Hallam also offered further details supporting Huntington's suspicions:

> She says soon after Capt. Potter received the letter from Mr. Lewis directing him to superintendent the work on the Light house Mr. Lester was over & requested to see the letter. Capt. Potter handed it to him — he read it & put it in his pocket & told Capt. Potter to take care of the old lighthouse as formerly & that Dr. [William] Hyde would superintendent the work on the new one. She recollects very well when her husband told her Mr. Lester had taken the letter from Mr. Lewis. She said to him she thought he had done wrong to let him have it.[47]

In short, Lester was now accused of intercepting I.W.P. Lewis's instructions to the builder and letting the building be constructed according to his own, or the builder's, slipshod standards, with the result that it was nearly uninhabitable and had been from its first day. Just how Pleasonton responded to this uproar is hard to determine; his side of the correspondence does not appear in the files. In any case, Smith and Brayton set to work and had it finished by July 2. They submitted a modest bill — $677.75. On August 29, Collector Huntington reported to Pleasonton, with evident satisfaction: "Agreeable to instructions, I have examined the Light House and property at Stonington, and have the honor to report that I believe it to be in good order in every respect & that the keeper is competent, and does her duties well."[48]

It remains a puzzle as to why John Bishop, a prolific and respected builder, many of whose structures remain part of the historic streetscape of New London, associated himself with such shabby work, or why the collector, Charles F. Lester, permitted, even insisted on, poor work badly done. Was it to permit one or both of them to set aside some of the money appropriated for the structure? There seem to be no further clues beyond Huntington's accusations, and they did not lead to legal action.

Huntington's reward was that often accorded the whistle-blower. On May 10, 1843, the New London *People's Advocate* reported: "We have to announce this week the removal of Wolcott Huntington, Esq., from the office of Collector this port, and the appointment of C.F. Lester, Esq., the former incumbent.... After remaining little more than a year, [Huntington] leaves none who knew him — and the circle is large — but sincerely regret his departure. . . .Mr. H. was furnished with no information respecting the causes of his removal — the official letter received by him merely stating the fact." Huntington largely vanished from public life after being ousted from the collectorship; it is not a surprise to read that he eventually died of apoplexy.[49]

A few days after Huntington left, Pleasonton wrote a letter to Lester blandly absolving him:

> Whatever complaints may have been made against you in connection with the Stonington Light, (and I do not now recollect any) made no impression on me, as I felt very confident that in erecting that building the fault was not with you, but with the plan of the building, drawn by young Lewis, who had no experience on the subject. The old roof which was flat and leaked was taken off and a raised roof substituted, since you left office, and now the building is dry and in good order. It affords me pleasure to state that you did nothing while formerly in office, in regard to the Light House Establishment, as well as I remember, which could impair my confidence in any degree.

Pleasonton's failure to remember Huntington's complaints against Lester represented a convenient oversight, because Huntington had threatened, in his correspondence with Pleasonton, to drag Lester into court.[50]

The argument over the Stonington lighthouse foreshadowed a dispute that came to be played out in a national arena. Indeed, the conversion of I.W.P. Lewis from an ally to an opponent of the Lighthouse Establishment was fed by his experience in Stonington. In a deposition of April 4, 1842, Lewis listed the Stonington lighthouse as one of several for which Pleasonton refused to pay his costs in fitting out the lanterns. Now the leading critic of his uncle Winslow and of Pleasonton, he was assigned by the Treasury Department on May 25, 1842, to report on the lighthouses of the East Coast.[51]

In January 1843, Lewis submitted to the secretary of the treasury his survey of the lighthouses of the Northeast, and the nature of his report made clear that he aimed at the removal of the Pleasonton regime: "The establishment of this country has languished under the rule of ignorant and avaricious contractors, unrestrained by any law or other influences requisite to the proper government of so important a branch of public service. It is to the want of such laws, as well as the absence of an active supervision of the details of the service, that we directly trace the present disordered and inefficient condition of the establishment."

Lewis took space in his report to discuss the loneliness, hardships, and poor pay of lighthouse keepers, and he might well have had the Potters in mind when he wrote:

> If the Government neglects to furnish keepers with what common humanity demands, it cannot be expected that this humble yet useful class of citizens should be so devoted to the discharge of their duties as if provided with homes that it would be their pride to maintain in perfect order and cleanliness. . . . Those who had a decent roof to cover their heads appeared industrious and happy, while those whose homes were in a state of partial ruin, who have a rickety lantern and apparatus to attend, a leaky roof over their beds at night . . . had a look of squalid wretchedness about them . . . . [52]

It might have seemed that Pleasonton was at last against the wall, but he and his ally Winslow Lewis fought back in the newspapers and in Congress, and somehow Pleasonton and his system survived. He was even able to terminate I.W.P. Lewis's survey before it was complete, and he had already seen to it that his ally, Charles Lester, who was dismissed by President Tyler, was reappointed by the same president, although the Senate avoided confirming the appointment. [53]

One of the few artifacts surviving of William Potter's life is a pocket watch with the back shown here. The engraving depicts Horta Harbor in the foreground across from Pico Island in the Azores. It might mean that Potter sailed to the Azores at some point, but it might have been a gift; sailors from the Azores were already settling in Stonington in the middle of the nineteenth century. *(Photograph by Mary Beth Baker)*

Patty Potter, Keeper

Although she was in her sixties when she succeeded her husband at the Stonington lighthouse, Patty Potter continued to serve for twelve years, into her mid-seventies. Her pay was $350 a year, fifty dollars more per annum than her husband's had been when he started and roughly the going rate on the Connecticut coast. Her nemesis, the collector Charles Lester, died in 1846; the new collector was Thomas Mussey of New London. Stonington, declared a port of entry, now had its own collector, but administration of Stonington's lighthouse remained in New London.[54]

When she asked Mussey to help her with a household problem, Mussey wrote to Pleasonton in her behalf on October 28, 1847:

> Mrs. P. Potter, keeper of the Light House at Stonington, has applied for a new cooking stove for the kitchen of that house. She informs me that she can procure one for $22 and sell the old one for ½ cent a pound or 75 cents, the difference being $21.25. Also one of coal to heat the Lantern, at $6.12. Mrs. P. would be pleased to get an early reply.

Pleasonton replied promptly enough, in a manner worthy of his fictional contemporary, Ebenzer Scrooge:

> Sir. Your letter of the 28th was received this morning. On referring to the contract for building the Stonington Light House, I was astonished to find that the Contractor was to furnish a cooking stove for the kitchen, a thing never done before. What the reason for it was does not appear. But the reason what it may be however there can be no allowance for a stove hereafter. If there be no chimney with a fire place there must be one made,

and the family must do their cooking in that. We might as well furnish the keeper with chairs, tables and every other article of furniture. . . . Pleasonton

Mussey obediently asked Patty Potter to obtain an estimate for building a cooking fireplace. Whether she did or made do is not known.[55]

Almost a year later occurred the exchanges that ever after darkened Patty Potter's name in lighthouse histories. In one book about women lighthouse

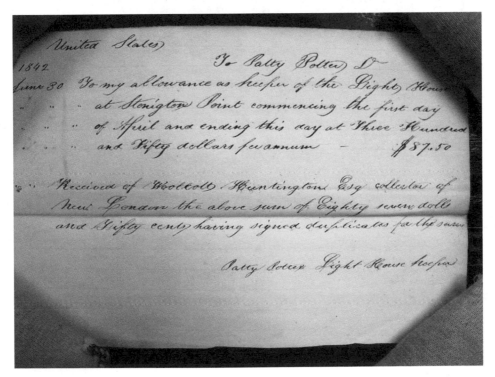

The first receipt for Patty Potter's pay as keeper of the Stonington light. Her husband died on May 10, 1842. *(Photographed by the authors at the National Archives, Washington)*

This newspaper fragment from February 3, 1847, reporting on the activities of the forty-ninth Congress, was found in 2013 pasted to a timber in the second floor of the Lighthouse. It appears to be a New London paper, part of whose title was Democrat. *(Photograph by Mary Beth Baker)*

keepers, the authors report that the "one piece of information remaining" about Patty Potter was that she "kept the most filthy lighthouse I [an unnamed lighthouse official] have ever visited; everything appears to have been neglected." In *The Lighthouses of Connecticut,* Jeremy D'Entremont quotes the same accusation, similarly unattributed, but notes that Patty Potter received a more favorable report in an inspection two years later.[56]

There is more to the story. On October 4, 1848, Fifth Auditor Pleasonton sent a letter to Collector Mussey, stating the following:

> Captain Howland in a report to me concerning the lights he has visited and supplied, states that Patty Potter, the keeper of the Stonington Light, keeps the most filthy house, he ever visited; that every thing appears to be neglected. As the goodness of a Light depends mainly on the keeper, you will inform Mrs. Potter that if I receive another complaint of the kind, altho' I am in favor of appointing widows of keepers to succeed them, I shall recommend her removal for I cannot tolerate neglect of this kind.[57]

Captain Jonathan Howland was a recipient of Pleasonton's favor, having been granted a monopoly in distributing whale oil to the nation's lighthouses. Why Patty Potter annoyed him became clear in her response to Collector Mussey, which he relayed to Pleasonton:

> Your letter of the 5th inst. was duly received and communicated the contents to Mrs. Potter. She excused herself by saying that Mr. Howland came along this year much earlier then he ever did before and that the family were sick and [she] had not cleaned up the House as usual; but she supposed the principal cause of his bad feeling towards her was occasioned by her complaining of the oil which he had brought her. She said she asked him why he did not bring her as good oil as he used to & the reply he made was, "You can not expect as good oil as you had formerly," when asked why she said he turned on his heal [sic] very abruptly and made no reply.
>
> I found the stairs much spotted with oil, and enquired the reason & was told it was owing to the bad construction of the lamps, they being made on the plan of Mr. Lewis, having no adjusting screws to prevent the oil from running over when it swells by reason of increased heat. In that particular I think the plan a bad one. As I perceived the inside of the tower was not as neat as it might be, I directed Mrs. Potter to have it white washed.[58]

In the summer of 1850, an inspector, evidently again Captain Howland, reported: "This building — for there is but one, the light being on the roof or on the tower connected with the house — we found in good order, except a little leaky. Lantern and lighting apparatus we found, as usual, in a neglected state. We put in a full set of iron burners." It was, at least, a passing grade and Patty Potter survived the threat to her job.[59]

She had a complaint of her own when, inexplicably, her pay failed to arrive in the final part of 1849, following the election of Zachary Taylor, who ushered in a Whig administration, replacing James Knox Polk's Democrats. After waiting nearly three months, she had her son Dyer write to the Fifth Auditor himself:

Oil had to be carried up this coil of steps to the fuel the lamps in the tower. This modern photo shows a railing installed after the Lighthouse became a museum. *(Photograph by Karl Walet of Savannah, used by permission)*

My mother Mrs. Potter Keeper of the Light House at this place has requested me to write you in regard to her salary for the third quarter of the year or the quarter ending Sept. 30 1849. She informs me that she has not as yet received her salary. That Mr. Mussey the late collector has written her that he had the money to pay with but that he had received no orders from you to pay it out as soon as he received his orders he would inform her. Upon inquiring I ascertained that the collector here had paid his subordinate the first of quarter. As she was alone[,] at her request I [have] taken the liberty to inform you of the circumstances.

Thinking there might be something wrong is my only apology for writing.

Indeed, Mussey, like many other Democratic appointees, was out as of September 1849. Apparently Patty Potter received her pay; there are no further such letters in the files. Less than a year later her son Dyer, already a widower after a marriage of less than two years, was dead of consumption at the age of 28, probably a victim of the dank home where he grew up.[60]

By 1851, the end was at last approaching for Stephen Pleasonton. In March, Congress approved a bill that created a lighthouse board made up of naval and military officers, as well as civil engineers and scientists. The board was directed to create a new system of governance for the lighthouse system. The board immediately interrogated Pleasonton, and found the replies unsatisfactory and vague. Pleasonton was given a second chance, but it was clear that his time was up. While there is no record that he was ever relieved of his title, fifth auditor, the lighthouse board had superseded him by 1852.

So ended an era of disgrace. Winslow Lewis, Pleasonton's old ally, died in 1850, and Pleasonton himself died in 1855. Their critic and antagonist, I.W.P. Lewis, who had crossed swords with them, also died in 1855, only in his forties. While Pleasonton and Winslow Lewis are almost unanimously execrated by later lighthouse historians, I.W.P Lewis, critic and engineer, has been hailed, on the basis of his critique of the old system and his construction of several major lighthouses, as a founder of America's modern lighthouse system.[61]

Patty Potter's final years at the lighthouse were saddened by the deaths of two more of her children. Eliza, evidently unmarried, died at the age of 43 in

October 1853. The youngest, Caroline, about 25 years old, died at the start of 1854. Now in her seventies, Patty Potter retired in the spring of the same year.

She went to live with her daughter Martha (also known as Patty); her husband, Stanton Sheffield, a ship carpenter; and their four children in the Sheffields' home at 85 Water Street in Stonington Borough. Durable as ever, she lived into her eighties. When she died in 1869, she left her goods to her four surviving daughters (one more son had predeceased her) and left $100 to the two eldest, Martha Sheffield and Sarah Harlow. The Potters' descendants lived in Stonington Borough well into the next century.[62]

Most of the Potter family is buried in the Stonington Cemetery at U.S. Route 1 and North Main Street. This large brownstone cross stands just east of the posts demarking the plot for the parents, William Potter and Patty Barker Potter. The name at the top is Jane Wilbur, a daughter-in-law, who died on April 4, 1848, at 23. The name of her husband, Dyer Barker Potter, was added below when he died two and a half years later, of consumption. *(Photograph by authors)*

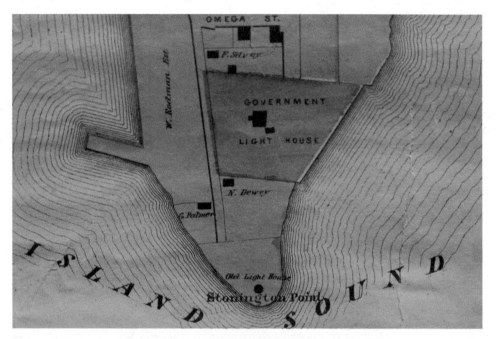

This map, drawn by an insurance company after 1840, shows that the first lighthouse continued to stand years after it was predicted that it would be swept into the sea.

After the Potters

The Potter era at Stonington's lighthouse lasted thirty years, a record not thereafter matched. In the remaining thirty-five years that the light remained lit, six keepers served, with only one lasting more than ten years. Patty Potter's successor, Luther Ripley, was another veteran (a private) of the War of 1812 and already in his sixties. Information about Ripley's pre-Stonington life indicates that he was appointed for political compatibility rather than maritime experience. He was an inlander, born in Windham, nearly fifty miles from the coast. Whether he had a trade is not known, but from the 1830s on he was active in minor public offices, such as justice of the peace, in the Windham County hamlet of Chaplin, and in activities of the local Democratic Party. Twice he was sent to Hartford as a representative in the state legislature.[63]

About 1843, Ripley became inspector of the port at Stonington, newly designated as a port of entry, at an annual salary of $500, substantial for those days. Two years later, a local newspaper reported that he had been removed from office, but official records do not note this action, and in 1849 he was still at work. A letter from his supervisor, Stonington port's collector, noted that Ripley's work had been arduous, requiring him to board 1,178 coasting vessels and seven foreign vessels in the most recent year. Early in 1850, Ripley prevailed upon Senator Hannibal Hamlin of Maine, then still a fellow Democrat (he was later a Republican vice-president), to oppose the appointment of Oliver York as collector of customs at Stonington, perhaps because Ripley himself had had his eye on the position. Ripley did not succeed in becoming collector and, it seems, lost his job as inspector as well, because the 1850 census listed him as having no occupation.[64]

He was appointed lighthouse keeper on April 19, 1854, at annual pay of $350, which would have been a sharp reduction had he not been able to install a large extended family in the rent-free lighthouse. The 1860 census shows Ripley living with a daughter, Emily; her husband, Henry B. Gardiner (of the famed Long Island Gardiners); their three children (one an infant of three months); and Ripley's son, John; John's wife, Sarah Macomber; and a "domestic," probably Sarah's sister Nancy — nine souls altogether. Luther Ripley's third wife, listed in the previous census, was no longer in the household.[65]

The most significant development at the lighthouse during Ripley's tenure was the replacement of the old-style parabolic reflector lights with, at last, a Fresnel lens in 1856, as directed by the Lighthouse Board. This was a sixth-order lens, the smallest manufactured, and standard for harbor lights. Even so, it was a vast improvement, casting a steady beam visible for as much as five miles. Ripley was also the first keeper appointed under the Lighthouse Board's new guide for keepers — elaborate, detailed instructions for cleaning and caring for the apparatus and the structure, but little or nothing on personal conduct.[66]

Ripley resigned on February 12, 1861. The date is significant; since Abraham Lincoln's election, seven states had seceded from the Union and Lincoln's inauguration was less than three weeks away. A few months after he left the lighthouse, Ripley revealed himself not only as a member of the opposition party but a "secesh" — a supporter of the new Southern confederacy. The *Boston Evening Transcript* described a tumultuous meeting in Borough Hall on August 9, 1861, chaired by Ripley, who sponsored resolutions condemning the four-month-old Civil War. To the surprise of Ripley and his faction, the resolutions failed and Ripley's group fled.[67]

Eventually, Ripley settled with his daughter Emily and her husband, Henry Gardiner, and five grandchildren in East Marion (Southold) on Long Island. A local paper described him as "plenty hale and hearty" and retaining "his mental as well as physical facilities." His service as a lighthouse keeper was not mentioned. He died in 1877, well into his eighties, and was buried in his home village, Chaplin.[68]

Ripley's immediate successor remains a puzzle. Winthrop Hand is listed as

Charles E.P. Noyes became keeper in 1869. Later he was keeper on the Eel Grass Ground light vessel, and in 1884 became the first keeper of the new Latimer Reef light, in Fishers Island Sound.

having been appointed on February 12, 1861, the day of Ripley's departure, and as being dismissed on April 12, 1861, the date that Fort Sumter was fired on. Who he was and why he left remain mysteries.[69]

Hand was followed by Henry Burgess, a native of Maryland and a ship rigger, according to the 1860 census. He appeared in the local newspapers in January 1867 as a witness to a murder that took place in the street just yards from the lighthouse. He testified that on November 23, 1866, he heard shots and that eventually his wife prevailed upon him to look outside, whereupon he found the body of one Rodman lying on Water Street. (The assailant was given five years.) He served until June 12, 1869, when he was removed, cause not explained. The census of 1880 indicates that he remained in Stonington, became a grocer, and lived on Main Street with his wife, Eliza. He died in 1894.[70]

The next keeper, Charles E. P. Noyes, spent much of his life on the water. Born in Stonington in 1831, he is recorded as being on a whaling voyage as a young man and serving as an ensign in the Union Navy during the Civil War. He and presumably his family — his wife, Mary Emma Langworthy, and two young daughters — moved into the lighthouse in June 1869, and remained a little more than three years, when he resigned to become the keeper of the light vessel at Eel Grass Ground, an obstacle in Fishers Island Sound two miles south and west of Stonington Borough. He went on one of the last whaling voyages out of Stonington in 1874 and 1875, then returned to the lightship, a hulk equipped with a nearly useless light. In 1884, he became the first keeper of the new Latimer Reef light, which can still be seen in Fishers Island Sound from Stonington Point; it lies on the New York side of the state line drawn through the water north of Fishers Island. Noyes remained as keeper there until 1909. In the end, he came ashore and died at the age of eighty-one in 1912.[71]

Pendleton Puts Out the Light

Captain Benjamin F. Pendleton was destined to preside over the last working days of the Stonington lighthouse. A member of one of Stonington's most notable seafaring dynasties, he was related to the Benjamin Pendleton who commanded the sealing expedition that had led to Nathaniel Palmer's discovery of Antarctica in 1820. He was a son of Harris Pendleton, a master mariner who built a house of bricks from ballast, which still stands on Main Street in the Borough. Frank Pendleton, as he was known, first sailed under his brother Gurdon; his last voyage was as master of the bark *Acquidnac* to Rio de Janeiro in 1866. He was forty-nine years old when appointed keeper in 1872, but in the 1880 census he continued proudly to list himself as a "Sea Captain." His acceptance of a post paying but $600 a year suggests that his voyages had enriched him but little; one descendant remembered that his wife, Mary Jane Cook, ran a shop in the Borough to sustain the family during his long voyages.

The 1870 census, just before his appointment, lists a family of nine, including the captain, his wife, and seven children, ranging in age from twenty-one years old down to two. By 1880, six children were living in the lighthouse, ten years older and obviously grown larger. Although tough and durable, the aging Captain Pendleton had apparently suffered a stroke and needed the help of his large family to carry out his duties. The youngest son, Frederick Starr Pendleton, years later remembered arising at dawn to climb up the tower and extinguish the lights and return to bed without opening his eyes, or so he claimed. Sons did not stay long, however, because a family rule evidently dictated that they should leave at the age of 18 and seek their fortune — which they did, successfully, notably in the insurance business in Brooklyn.[72]

Even before Captain Pendleton's appointment, planning was under way that led to the dousing of the Stonington light. A report by the Corps of Engineers recommended in 1871 the construction of a jetty running southeast from Wamphassuc Point, on the west shore of the harbor, and the removal of the old breakwater on the east shore. That plan was modified: The old breakwater would stay in place, and a new breakwater would be extended straight east toward it from the opposite shore. At the same time dangerous Penguin Shoal, parallel to the western shore, would be dredged. The dredging took place, but the breakwater was deferred.[73]

This photograph is believed to show Captain Benjamin Franklin Pendleton and two family members, including his wife, Mary Jane Cook, and a daughter. They are standing outside the Lighthouse, probably in the 1880's.

Before the breakwater across Penguin Shoal could be started, the Borough came to life. The governing Warden and Burgesses, and eighty-four residents, filed a remonstrance against the plan for a breakwater at Penguin Shoal on grounds that traffic to the upper harbor would be constricted. Instead, the Boroughites declared, a breakwater should be built at Wamphassuc Shoal, to the south, and the old breakwater dismantled and rebuilt farther down at Windmill Point, more or less pointing toward Wamphassuc. In response a summit of officers from the Corps of Engineers met in Stonington on June 29, 1875, at the Wadawanuck Hotel. They boarded a tug and inspected the waters, then sent to Washington a plan to build a breakwater 2,000 feet long, angled south and east from Wamphassuc Point, thus creating a harbor of refuge on its lee side. That breakwater was completed five years later, and another to the east and south, which came to be known as the outer breakwater, was completed in the 1890s.[74]

The Providence & Stonington Steamboat Company soon placed on the new inner breakwater a light to show the way into Stonington Harbor. This act, and similar measures in other ports, annoyed the Lighthouse Board in Washington, which said that such lights were not consistently maintained and confused mariners. The unauthorized lights were also, it appeared, sometimes brighter than the government lights. In 1888, the board decided that a government light and fog signal should be put on the breakwater in place of the private signal. Moreover, the board announced that "in consequence of the completion of the breakwater at the entrance of this harbor, the present light has ceased to be of any practical use as an aid to navigation." When the new signal was finished, the board said, "The present light will be discontinued."[75]

The old light went dark on November 1, 1889. The new signal was a 25-foot tower, showing a steady red light, planted atop the eastern end of the western breakwater. The keeper was obliged to stay there at night to tend the light and in foggy weather to sound the warning bell. The old lighthouse now became only a residence for keepers and their families. Although the distance from the shore to the breakwater light — estimated at five-eighths of a mile — was not great, in the wrong season or weather it was a trial for the elderly keepers to get to their post, or to return from it.[76]

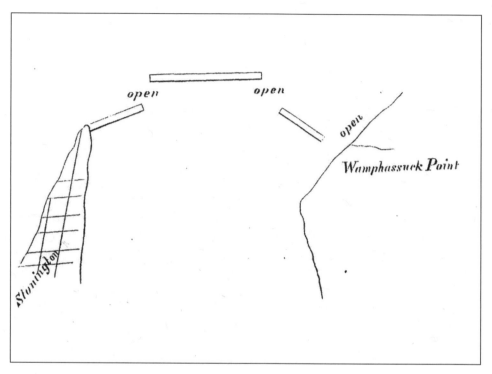

Preliminary drawing by the Corps of Engineers in 1871 for constructing new breakwaters to shield Stonington harbor. It was one of a number of schemes that were discarded before the west and east breakwaters were built outside the harbor.

Captain Pendleton evidently chose not to stay on the job of keeping the break-water light; he retired. Other seafarers followed him as keepers, although their exact order and periods of service are not entirely clear. One, Captain Samuel D. Pendleton (evidently not part of Captain Benjamin Pendleton's family) was not called a keeper, but a "light tender." He did not live in the old lighthouse, and was evidently an employee of the Corps of Engineers. He was responsible for fueling the light on the west end of the long and more distant east breakwater, which had been built to impede the rush of storms up the gap between Napatree Point and Fishers Island. Although Samuel Pendleton did not have to sail or row the mile out to the light every day, the responsibility was enough to earn him pay of $40 a month and a sympathetic story in the New London *Day*.[77]

Captain Benjamin Franklin Pendleton and two granddraughters, Laura and Marian. An inscription on the back of the photo says "c. 1907." By then Pendleton, the last keeper of the lighthouse light, was retired. He died in 1909.

THE BREAKWATER KEEPERS

The first keeper of the west breakwater lighthouse, Captain George W. Beckwith, was the next occupant of the old lighthouse. He was called "captain" as a courtesy; in fact he was a ship's steward, who had spent twenty years at sea after serving briefly in the Civil War. He was one of the assistant keepers of the Penfield Reef Light, off Fairfield, Connecticut, before coming to Stonington in 1890. As he passed the age of fifty in the mid-nineties, he was troubled by rheumatism and found the job less and less to his liking. He called on Captain Lemuel Staplin, of Stonington, to spell him, and Staplin was in charge when the United States military constructed a gun emplacement behind the west breakwater and set up an encampment on the lighthouse grounds early in the Spanish-American War .

As winter approached at the end of 1898, Beckwith announced his plan to resign, citing his ailments and such hardships as having to hike to the breakwater light when the water passage was too rough or was frozen; this meant a trek north through the Borough and down Wamphassuc Point to the far side of the breakwater and across its top to the lighthouse, a distance of two-plus miles. But he did not arrange his rotation with Staplin shrewdly; in February 1899 he had to reach the light during a storm and was stranded there several days in zero weather.[78]

His successor was Captain Joseph J. Fuller, famed for his perilous adventures in the southern seas in pursuit of elephant seals, which he recounted in his reminiscences, published years after his death under the title *Master of Desolation*. "Desolation" was the name American sailors gave Kerguelen, a bleak

This twenty-five-foot lighthouse was planted atop the east end of the new breakwater at the entrance to the harbor. When it was lighted, the old Lighthouse went dark, on November 1, 1889. In this situation, the keeper had to remain on the breakwater at night and in fog to sound the warning bell. The artist, Reynolds Beal, also sketched the skyline of Stonington Borough on the same pad. The drawing is dated July 18, 1899.

archipelago; in 1880, Fuller was shipwrecked there with twenty sailors for almost a year. He had been born on another remote island, the British-held Tristan da Cunha, to an American sailor and a daughter of the honorary governor. Eventually the family moved to New England and at 19 Joseph made his first voyage to Desolation, on a whaler. After a pause for naval service in the Civil War, he went to sea again; all told, he is recorded as working sixteen voyages out of New London, twelve of them as master. He retired as a skipper in 1895.

But he did not rest. When the Spanish-American War started in 1898, he went as a keeper to the perilous Race Rock light, off the western tip of Fishers Island, thence to Sakonnet Light in Rhode Island, and then, in late 1899, to Stonington. Fuller, nearly sixty, had the doubtful privilege of being the last keeper to live in the old lighthouse, with his wife, who was from New London, and three semi-grown children. He also had the added burden of tending the lights on both breakwaters, the responsibility having been transferred from the Corps of Engineers to the Lighthouse Board.[79]

In the meantime as he aged, Captain Fuller found his work occasionally burdensome. In 1908, a storm smashed his little boat on a rock and he had to attract the attention of his family by waving his coat; a powerboat was sent out and saved him from having to spend the night in the cold. On another occasion, the light on the eastern breakwater, which was hung from a stick, was blown off, but he could not get there to repair it. And once his launch filled with rainwater and sank. However, he remained on the job for ten years more. Meanwhile, mindful of his role as a public figure, he spoke to local groups such as the Boy Scouts about his adventures on faraway Desolation.[80]

There was hope of a better keeper's dwelling, if the Fullers could show patience. For several years, the Lighthouse Board and the Department of the Treasury had been deploring the condition of the old lighthouse as a residence:

> This Department has the honor to state, at the instance of the Lighthouse Board, that a recent inspection of the Stonington Breakwater, Connecticut, light-station has shown that its keeper's dwelling is in a condition so unhealthful as to menace the lives of its occupants, there

The Fuller family in front of the Lighthouse, which was their home for several years before the new keeper's house was built.

Captain Joseph J. Fuller (1840-1920) and his wife,
about 1910, on the steps of the new keeper's house.

The house the government built in 1908 for the keeper and family, south of the Lighthouse. This building has been assimilated by the growth of the twentieth-century Point House.

having been more or less sickness in every family residing therein during the past twenty years. The house is very old, no work has been done on it for a long time, it is past economical repair, and it is in such a condition of deterioration as to make it almost uninhabitable. The Board at its session on November 4, 1901, considered the question of remedying this unsanitary condition, and concluded that the dwelling is past economical repair and that the erection of a small modern dwelling for the keeper is therefore an urgent necessity. It is estimated that such a dwelling can be built for a cost not exceeding $6,000.

This Department concurs with the Light-House Board as to the necessity for providing this keeper's dwelling at the Stonington Breakwater, Connecticut light-station, and recommends that an appropriation of $6,000 be made therefor.

This was a clear enough statement of the need, but the new keeper's dwelling was put off year after year. Funds were finally appropriated in 1906, and the

Stonington Mirror reported on June 3, 1908, that the house, built on open space only feet south of the old lighthouse, was started. It was a square, shingled two-story dwelling with a wide front porch, facing Water Street. The Fullers were at last able to move in and they posed happily on the front steps. Finally, in April 1918, Captain Fuller retired; he died in New London in 1920, saluted as the last of his breed.[81]

The final keeper of the breakwater lights was Louis S. Poutray, a landscaper by profession who signed up with the lighthouse service when he failed to qualify for the military during World War I. With his wife, teenage daughter, mother-in-law, and niece, he moved into the keeper's house and took up his duties of fueling the East Breakwater light and rowing out to the little sparkplug lighthouse on the West Breakwater to spend the night. His daughter, interviewed decades later, remembered the years at Stonington Point fondly. Poutray used the vacant federal land south of the keeper's house to tend flourishing gardens. His daughter attended the Borough School and, an only child, made friends with the family across the street with a big record collection, in a house where DuBois beach lies now. When the breakwater light was automated, Louis Poutray worked briefly at the Latimer Reef lighthouse, then retired and died in 1931 at the age of 55. His widow died on Napatree Point during the 1938 hurricane. His daughter lived until 2003, attaining the age of 98.[82]

The lighthouse in 1914, during one of its winters as a bleak derelict. The new keeper's house, to the left, was built in 1908 and for the first time the Lighthouse was vacant. Note lobster traps in foreground. The inscription on the back of the snapshot reads, "With the compliments of Herbert Francis Sherwood 21 Feb. 1914" *(Photograph courtesy of Henry Robinson Palmer III)*

Stonington's Motif No. 1:

A Portfolio of Views of the Lighthouse

L ike Gloucester's famous "Motif No. 1"—the fishing shack favored by generations of artists—Stonington's Lighthouse has attracted artists and photographers for decades. The portfolio offered in these pages provides a sampling from hundreds of images by professional and amateur, young and old.

NEW YORK DAILY GRAPHIC AUG. 26, 1873

This sketch of the Lighthouse, dated August 26, 1873, was published in the *Daily Graphic* in New York. The area to the south is not yet densely developed, but has sheds and wharves for fishing.

Anonymous drawing of the Lighthouse, dated 1880, shows the wooden ell in the rear. The artist has coded the sketch for adding color later, "bk" for black and "w" for white.

Picture of the Borough skyline, centered on the Lighthouse, sketched by the local artist Reynolds Beal, dated July 18, 1899.

The Lighthouse, now serving only as the keeper's residence, about 1890, in the period when the Lighthouse was whitewashed.

The area around the Lighthouse about 1890 showing kitchen gardens and other household activities. The spiky tower is an early one, used to display storm warnings. *(Courtesy Henry Robinson Palmer III)*

Old postcard photographed from the rip-rap on the Point shows three kids on the seawall.

Postcard dated May 22, 1906, shows the Lighthouse in its whitewash although it was about to be left vacant.

A Boston commercial photographer, A.E. Alden of 63 Court Street, took this photo of the Lighthouse, probably with a plate camera, sometime after the light was doused in 1889 and the lamp removed from the lantern. Alden's motto, printed with his name on the back of the mounting cardboard, was "Views Made to Order." The name Palmer & Co., Stonington, Ct., is stamped below. *(© Howard G. Park III, formerly in the collection of Henry R. Palmer Jr.)*

Photograph of the Lighthouse ell shows a chimney there, indicating the area may have been used for a kitchen, but the building is probably now uninhabitated.

View of the Lighthouse after the Keeper's House was built in 1908 shows gardens, stone walls, places for domestic animals and other neighborhood activity. *(Courtesy Henry Robinson Palmer III)*

STONINGTON HISTORICAL SOCIETY

XMAS   1927

1 Try *zinc plate* process
2 *sharper litho* people
3 Photo + *printed on heavy sepia paper*

To be made into
cards to be sold
for benefit of Society

Mrs E. P. York
STONINGTON
Conn

Miss A. F. Mason
31 Grace Court Brooklyn
Will call $4.42

N⁵/₈ 16466

Design signed by C.F. Gould, a commercial artist, for a card to be used by the Stonington Historical Society for the first Christmas after it opened the Lighthouse to the public. No evidence is
available that it was completed or used. View on facing page shows notations by the artist and
others. *(Collection of Howard G. Park, used by permission)*

Painting by Philip Littell is titled "On Front Street." It shows the neighborhood of the Lighthouse in the early nineteen-seventies. The view is down the west side of south Water Street looking toward the parking lot at the Point. The nearest house was Nanny's Doghouse (which served ice cream) and the most distant one was the Joseph house, which adjoined duBois Beach. Both are now gone. The Lighthouse sign shows at the left edge. *(Used with permission of Alyssa Littell Storrow, the artist's sister)*

Left: Boarded for the season, the Lighthouse stands sharp and clear in the winter light in this portrait by the distinguished photographer Rollie McKenna, who specialized in portraits of literary figures and scenes of Stonington Borough.

The Stonington Band on the front façade of the Lighthouse, probably in the nineteen-thirties. This group, once called the Imperial Band, was formed by the Portuguese musicians who lived in the Lighthouse area—South of the Cannons, as it was often called.

The Joseph house, which was on Water Street across from the Lighthouse in the nineteen-seventies, showing the curving Lighthouse walkway. *(Photo by authors)*

The 1997 Fourth of July picnic on the Lighthouse grounds, sponsored by the South of the Cannons community group. *(Photo by authors)*

STONINGTON LIGHT
BUILT 1840

An early rubber stamp for visitors' use as a souvenir, created from a drawing by Sibby Lynch. The black stamp was used later to validate visits by members of the U.S. Lighthouse Society, founded in 1983. This version was standarized to fit into a space in the Lighthouse Society's "passport."

STONINGTON POINT LIGHTHOUSE CT

Stonington Historical Society

A student work from 2012 shows the continuing attraction of the Lighthouse to local artists. This was painted by Julia Royer while a senior in the Stonington High School. She was taking the Local/Regional Studies class taught by Jennifer Norcross and elected to paint the picture as a project for extra credit. *(Courtesy Julia Royer and Jennifer Norcross)*

View of the Lighthouse tower by the photographer and writer Raymond Uzanas of Stonington, taken from Stonington Commons, distant several hundred yards. *(Courtesy Raymond Uzanas)*

Stonington photographer John Papp caught the autumn moon rising behind the Old Lighthouse Museum on October 4, 2009, when he went out to get a picture of a rainbow over Salt Acres. *(© Copyright 2013 John Papp, used by permission)*

Buying a Lighthouse

With the departure of Captain Fuller and his family, the old lighthouse became a derelict, used only for miscellaneous storage. But after only a year or so of vacancy, the first hint of a new function surfaced. The Stonington Historical and Genealogical Society had been founded in 1895 in the customary way: Stonington gentry, many bearing names passed down from early settlers — Noyes, Chesebrough, Palmer, Stanton — formed a club to talk about ancestors and local history. In its early years, the Society, few in number, met quarterly to hear papers; it also collected genealogies and family Bibles. When the new Stonington Free Library building at Wadawanuck Square in Stonington Borough opened in 1900, a Historical Society room was earmarked, and as late as 1955 the Society was paying the library a modest sum for meeting there and for storing its books.

By 1909 the Society had begun to think of expansion. The meeting of August 1909, attended by twenty-two members, voted to place historical plaques on early settlers' houses. The *Stonington Mirror* also reported: "A new home for the historical society was discussed and [it was] suggested that the old lighthouse building would make a most desirable location. Steps have already been taken to this end." No such steps were recorded subsequently, in part because the Society apparently kept no minutes from 1911 to 1913.[83]

The question was destined to come up again. The members of the Society were keenly aware of the approach of the centennial of the 1814 Battle of Stonington, when Stonington's cannons, still on display in a Borough square, drove off a British naval squadron. The observances customarily displayed the

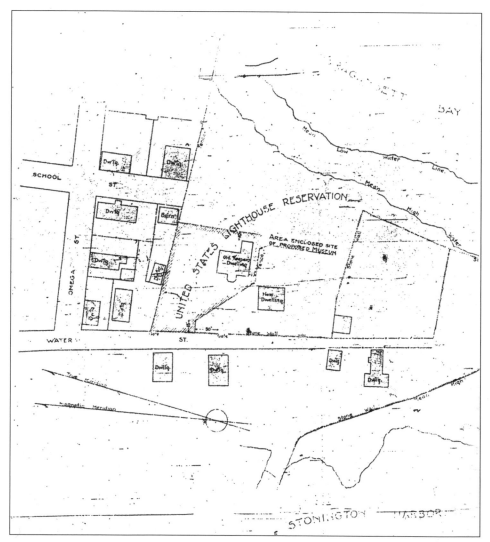

This diagram from 1913 shows the area the government wanted fenced off in the event the Historical Society took a lease on the Lighthouse. It did not.

chief artifact of the battle, the battered and pierced battle flag, nine feet by seventeen, older than the Star Spangled Banner. Francis Amy, who served in Captain Potter's militia company during the battle, became custodian of the flag afterward; when he died in 1863, it passed to another veteran, Nathan G. Smith. After the founding of the Historical Society, Smith's daughter Caroline eventually — probably about 1900 — turned the precious relic over to the Society. In 1909, sere and ragged, it was photographed while displayed hanging from the windows of a private home.[84]

The centennial program called not only for display of the old flag but of the 250-year-old town's other artifacts. As its part of the observance, the Historical Society was asked to take charge of "collecting and exhibiting historical objects in connection with the 1914 celebration." Searching for exhibit space, the Society made inquiries about the lighthouse. On July 7, 1913, G.R. Putnam, commissioner of the Bureau of Lighthouses, which had succeeded the old Lighthouse Board three years before, answered an inquiry from Henry R. Palmer, secretary of the Society. Putnam offered a revocable five-year rent-free lease for the lighthouse, to be used as a museum — with conditions, such as building a fence to protect the keeper's house. On July 29, J.T. Yates, a federal lighthouse inspector, wrote to ask Palmer to identify parties to a possible agreement. He enclosed a drawing showing the area the government wanted fenced in.[85]

On November 5, 1913, the Society held its first on-the-record meeting in two years. Dr. James H. Weeks, a dentist, was chosen president. Then the meeting discussed the government offer and appointed a committee. Two months later the New London *Day* reported that Weeks had inspected the old lighthouse and had found it "altogether unsuitable" for the proposed use and damp and leaky besides. The annual meeting in February confirmed this view. The lighthouse was not to be part of the centennial, and the government offer was not pursued.[86]

The Society's centennial exhibition was offered in the summer and fall of 1914 in Ryon's Hall, a former church at the corner of Water and Pearl streets in Stonington Borough. In a way, the lighthouse was present in Ryon's Hall. The tireless host and curator was Captain Edward H. Sheffield, known as Captain Sheff. He was a grandson of the first and second keepers of the Stonington

Captain Edward H. Sheffield (c. 1838-1923) was a grandson of the first two keepers, William Potter and Patty Potter. As the host of the Ryon's Hall display in 1914, he was hugely popular.

Marking the centennial of the Battle of Stonington, the display in Ryon's Hall was a crowded hodgepodge of objects, some owned by the Historical Society and many lent or given by other organizations and private people. Much of it became the core of the Lighthouse Museum's collection.

Harbor Lighthouse, Captain William Potter and his widow and successor, Patty Potter. The Widow Potter lived with her son-in-law Stanton Sheffield, her daughter Martha (Patty) Potter, and her grandchildren until she died in 1869. Captain Sheff had grown up while his grandmother was keeper and no doubt learned maritime lore at her knee. He declined any compensation for his work, and was given a gold watch by the organizing committee. He might have served as an ideal host at the lighthouse had he survived until its reopening, but he died in 1923.[87]

Many historical items, valuable and otherwise, were lent for the three-month display, and later some were given outright to the Society. More than a few, including the torn battle jacket of militiaman John Miner, a number of cannon balls, and a complete Congreve rocket, are still centerpieces of the Society's collections. However, the chief artifact of the battle, the great Battle Flag, was not displayed in Ryon's Hall, although it was in possession of the Society. Held aloft by two youths, descendants of the battle's hero, Jeremiah Holmes, it was rolled through the Borough streets on a wagon as part of the pageant parade, then returned to storage. The official account of the celebration stated: "So complete was the success of the exhibition that a great impetus was given to the proposal for a suitable home for the Society, in which a permanent collection of historical objects might be displayed."[88]

But during and after the Great War, the Historical Society declined into quiescence, and Henry R. Palmer, who had been active in the centennial observances, called it "a recently useless institution." So uncertain did its future seem that Dr. Charles Mallory Williams, in behalf of the Society, wrote in 1917 to the Society for Preservation of New England Antiquities to ask whether it would be willing to become custodian of the Stonington Society's collections. The preservation society said no.[89]

The search for a home finally resumed in 1924. In response to his inquiry, Dr. Williams received a letter from H.B. Bowerman, acting commissioner of lighthouses:

> 1. Referring to your letter of April 21, 1924, relative to the desire of the Stonington Historical Society to rent the Stonington Point Lighthouse Reservation:
> 2. You are respectfully informed that this matter is under consideration and that you will be further advised in regard thereto at an early date.[90]

On May 2, a new acting commissioner, J.S. Conway, wrote to say that "consideration is now being given to the sale of this lighthouse, and it is therefore not considered advisable to rent the property at this time." Williams was assured he would get a chance to bid. In October, Dr. Williams nudged the Bureau of Lighthouses again about "hiring or buying" the property. Conway replied promptly:

> I beg to advise you that this Service intends to make a survey and complete the work of building the necessary fence to separate the part of the reservation that is to be retained from that to be sold so that the lighthouse, together with the property on which it is located, can be sold during

the coming winter or early spring. It will be necessary for this property to be sold by competitive bids. . . . When the date . . . has been fixed . . . you may submit a bid.[91]

In the meantime, Henry R. Palmer was trying to resurrect an organization able to take the lighthouse project in hand. On August 4, 1924, he wrote to the lawyer J. Culbert Palmer of New York that "we want your influence to reorganize the Stonington Historical Society." He went on: "You are aware of the situation, of course. . . . For ten years we have talked of what ought to be done and for ten years we have done nothing. Surely we don't want to let it go as it is for ten years more."

Palmer subsequently reported that a caucus of eight had met and appointed him to ask Culbert Palmer to become president. He added: "We ought to push the scheme of a permanent home for the society and actually get installed there in order to secure as soon as possible the many valuable relics and souvenirs that are only awaiting our possession of safe quarters." He received a letter from Culbert Palmer declining, but there must have been further negotiations because Culbert Palmer in fact became president at the August annual meeting.[92]

The Society met again on December 29, 1924. The minutes record that Mrs. Frank F. Dodge (Anne Atwood), "the chair of the committee on procuring a home for the Society," reported that "in the estimations of the committee, the Light House at the Point would provide a suitable home for the Society and that it could be put in order with very little expense." The president said he had been told that the lighthouse would be offered for sale in the spring. The meeting voted to continue the committee "with power to formulate a plan for the raising of the money for the purchase of the Light House and an Endowment fund." An appeal was drafted seeking gifts toward a $25,000 endowment fund. There is no evidence that the Society accumulated an endowment until many years later.[93]

On February 7, 1925, Anne Atwood Dodge wrote to Williams that private investors wanted to buy the lighthouse to start a tearoom there but would not bid against the Society. The outsiders' idea of a good bid was $3,500, she wrote, although the government agent "thought $10,000!" The idea of a tearoom at the lighthouse was to prove persistent, even indelible.[94]

Henry Robinson Palmer (1867-1943) invested great effort to get the Society to move beyond being "a recently useless institution." *(Courtesy of Henry Robinson Palmer III)*

Eugene Atwood (1846-1926), president of the Atwood Machine Company on Water Street, advanced the money so the Historical Society could buy the Lighthouse in 1925. *(Engraving from* History of Eastern Connecticut, *1931)*

In April, Commissioner Conway wrote Williams that bids would be opened at the office of the superintendent of lighthouses on Staten Island, New York, on May 14. This brought a burst of activity. On May 12, two days before the deadline, a bid of $3,650 was submitted by Eugene Atwood, father of Anne Atwood Dodge and owner of the Atwood Machine Company on Water Street. It was accompanied by a letter from Williams, as treasurer of the Society: "The attached bid for the old lighthouse property at Stonington, Conn., is submitted by Mr. Atwood for the benefit of the Stonington Historical Society. If Mr. Atwood secures the property, the Society intends to put the old lighthouse in order and to maintain it as an architectural monument and as a museum where objects of historical interest can be displayed." The way was paved for this letter by an appeal from Representative Richard P. Freeman, the Second District's member of Congress, asking the commissioner of lighthouses to permit sale to a private person. The commissioner responded that he would consider this since the property would be used by the Historical Society for "patriotic or semi-public purposes."[95]

Representative Freeman then received a letter from the acting commissioner on May 23 saying that the "successful bidder" was Eugene Atwood. In fact, Atwood was the only bidder, as the Society had already learned from Charles H. Simmons*, president of John Simmons Co., a metal factor in New York City, in a note to Culbert Palmer on May 19:

> I suppose you are aware of the outcome of the bidding on the lighthouse property. Mr. Atwood's was the only bid. Just before I left on Thursday last Charlie Williams called me up and asked me to follow this up, and I find that the only bid, as aforesaid, was the one Mr. Atwood submitted for $3650. This has been sent to Washington and whether or not it will be accepted, we cannot tell until we are advised from there.
>
> It seems too bad that you have to pay that much, as it could no doubt have been bought for less. Mr. Atwood says the property is not worth that much but he was encouraged to put in the bid for that amount.[96]

---

* Charles Simmons was the grandfather of Robert R. Simmons of Stonington, much later a Connecticut representative in Congress.

Plaque in the entryway under the tower reads: "This Lighthouse, which became the permanent home of the Stonington Historical Society in 1925, stands today in its altered form a fitting tribute to the devoted service & unerring taste of J. Culbert Palmer president & Edward Palmer York architect."

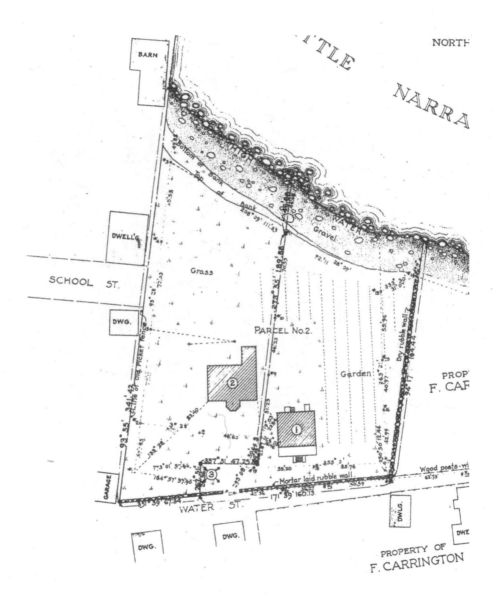

This plan shows the contour and placement of the land the government reserved for its Weather Bureau tower (marked No. 3 on map) when it sold the Lighthouse to the Stonington Historical Society.

Markers were placed by the government to show property retained for Weather Bureau use for its tower and signals. These stones continued in place into the twenty-first century. When the Historical Society in 2012 began research on rehabilitating the Lighthouse, the government acknowledged that it had never relinquished the strip. However, neither had it protested nearly a century of use by the Historical Society and the public.

The official forms used in soliciting such tenders include the caveat that the government may reject any and all bids. It seems possible that an inside source had let the Society know the minimum amount the government would accept, and that was what Atwood offered. By the deadline, the government certainly knew there was not to be a bidding war. The deed, in favor of Atwood, was conveyed on June 8, 1925.[97]

On July 17, 1925, a special Society meeting was called, and the minutes show that forty-two members responded. Two linked items were on the agenda: the securing of the lighthouse as "a permanent home" and the incorporation of the society. First, Edward Palmer York, a partner in the prestigious York & Sawyer architectural firm of New York City, moved "that the Association purchase the Lighthouse property from Mr. Eugene Atwood at cost and expenses to him, and that the officers of the association be authorized to consummate the transaction, using the funds of the Association and raising additional funds for the purpose." This was carried, followed by a motion of thanks to Atwood.

Albert Mason moved and Henry R. Palmer seconded the other action of the meeting: "That the Association be incorporated under the name of the Stonington Historical Society and that a committee consisting of the officers together with three additional members, to be appointed by the President, be directed to take charge of the details of the purchase from Mr. Atwood, and of the incorporation and reorganization of the Society." Adopted, adjourned. Presumably the new corporation would have better legal status than a mere club to own and manage property.[98]

The annual meeting of the Society was held on September 25, 1925, at the Stonington Free Library, with J. Culbert Palmer presiding. The fundraising committee was thanked for more than covering the cost of the purchase. Then Louise Trumbull, secretary pro tem, wrote: "The committee was dismissed and The Historical and Genealogical Society dissolved." Immediately afterward, the same people convened as a new corporate entity, the Stonington Historical Society Incorporated. On September 30, the new corporation presented its check for $3,650 to Atwood's secretary, who delivered the deed to the Society's president.*[99]

* Less than a year later, Eugene Atwood died at his home in New York at the age of eighty.

On October 25, 1925, the Society had a plot drawn of its first real property. It showed a trapezoid of land between lower Water Street and Little Narragansett Bay with a notch at the southwest corner, which was property retained by the government for its weather mast. The north boundary, from the high-water mark in the bay to Water Street, was 341 feet long. The south boundary, from high water to the government notch, was 236 feet. The government plot, measuring 26 feet east to west at its widest and 47 feet north to south along the street, embraced the opening in the wall for the path to the Lighthouse. This meant that the Society's primary access to its Lighthouse was a right-of-way over government land and a possible source of distant trouble.[100]

This portrait of the lighthouse was painted in 1925 by 20-year-old Sara Emily Darrell, daughter of a local family, who was taking art instruction. The artist, who was by then Sara Emily Darrell Atwood Cottrell, died in 1989; her granddaughter, Erica Lindberg Gourd, gave permission for use of the picture. © ELG Stonington Originals ™, 2001

SAVED FOR WHAT?

At last, it appeared, the lighthouse had been saved from abandonment. But the question was: saved for what? In the summer of 1925, Emily Darrell, a young woman from Stonington and New York, painted a picture of the lighthouse, showing it with a green lawn and a tree in full leaf — the lighthouse in its last moments before being put to new uses. The building is totally recognizable to all those who have worked or visited there over the last eighty-odd years; what it omits is the actual prospects the Historical Society may have found when it first occupied its new property.[101]

The Historical Society's leaders, most of them New York men who summered in Stonington, were largely devoid of museum experience. They did not look beyond refurbishing the building and grounds and placing the Society's accumulated artifacts under its roof. They showed no particular interest in the lighthouse as a historic structure — why it was there or who had worked there. They could be excused, however; there were no immediately useful precedents available for creating a museum at a lighthouse. This was evidently the first of its type. Of course, other historic buildings, including some of New England's plethora of old houses, had shifted into new uses as galleries and museums. But could a lighthouse be a museum? The Society took years before it began to realize such a prospect.[102]

Yet the opportunities were always there for utilizing what the lighthouse itself had to offer. Popular fiction cast a romantic haze over lighthouses. In 1890, Laura E. Richards, the daughter of Julia Ward Howe, published a weepy short novel, *Captain January*, that became a huge seller, reprinted well into the twentieth century. Captain January, retired from seafaring, keeper of a lighthouse in Maine, rescues and rears a child from a shipwreck. He calls her Star Bright, giving her an education based on a complete Shakespeare and the Bible. A Victorian orphan tale, but the vigilant and lonely keeper in a storm-swept dwelling seized imaginations.[103]

Lighthouse keepers were known as salty raconteurs, hosts who told the curious of foundering vessels and perilous rescues. The government was aware of this interaction; among the instructions to keepers in 1881 is this:

> Keepers must be courteous and polite to all visitors who conform to the regulations, and show them everything of interest about the station at such times as it will not interfere with their lighthouse duties. Keepers must not allow visitors to handle the apparatus or deface light-house property. Special care must be taken to prevent the scratching of names or initials on the glass of the lanterns or on the windows of the towers. No visitor should be admitted to the tower unless attended by a keeper . . . . Keepers must not make any charge, nor receive any fee, for admitting visitors to light-houses.

Still, keepers traditionally sold mementos and were tipped for giving tours, which surely helped augment their deplorable pay. One not insignificant advantage for Stonington: the lighthouse, unlike many, was accessible by foot rather than isolated on a pier or distant outcropping. But the Old Lighthouse Museum, as it came to be called, was not destined to have a caretaker of the kind Captain Sheff might have been, nor did the Society's governors initially place special value on possible links with Stonington's maritime past.[104]

The Historical Society at least set about cleaning up. The iron framework around the light was mended without charge by the Atwood Machine Company. The painting and installation of the glass was carried out by one E. A. Potter at a "greatly reduced cost" of $39.58. Attention was also directed to the grounds; a blueprint of the lighthouse property was to be "distributed to the Stonington Garden Club to elicit competitive plans for improvement."[105]

The minutes reveal an unanticipated problem. The north property line marked the boundary with the heavily populated Portuguese neighborhood of that day. Census records show that the chockablock houses on Hancox, Omega, School, Trumbull and south Water streets sheltered large families with many children. The abandoned lighthouse grounds no doubt had provided an inviting play-

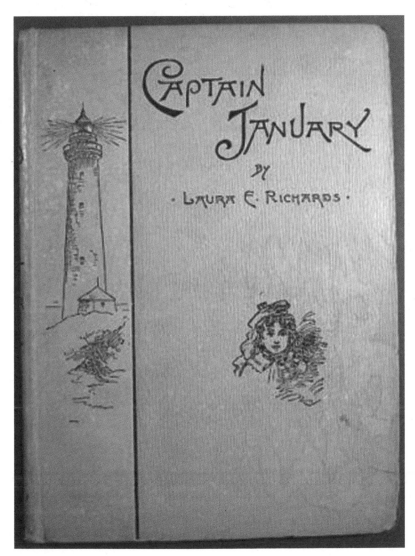

Captain January, a popular Victorian novel published in 1890, endowed lighthouse keepers with a reputation for courage and kindness. It was reprinted well into the twentieth century and was filmed twice.

Edward Palmer York (1865-1928) is shown here with his family at "The Hill," in Stonington Borough. A New York architect, he drew the plan to adapt the Lighthouse as a museum for the Historical Society. *(Photograph courtesy of Anna North Coit)*

ground. The minutes reported: "The chair of the Grounds Committee reported that the wire netting loaned by Mrs. Carrington had been put up to protect the property on the north side, and that no-trespassing signs had been placed in position." Of course, that was no real solution.[106]

By the time the annual meeting of the Society was held on July 9, 1926, almost a year had passed since acquisition of the lighthouse, but planning had not advanced far. The minutes note a report by T. W. Cutler, the registrar: "The property of the Society which had been stored under the Second Congregational Church had been moved to the Lighthouse." Then Edward Palmer York, who headed the building committee, offered suggestions for moving ahead. For example, the light in the first floor was inadequate, he said, and should be improved with new windows. When the governors met on August 20, York provided offered two specific plans: The governors authorized him to proceed with the blueprints for "Scheme A" and to employ a builder to remove partitions, put on a new roof, make the structure weather-tight and make "necessary repairs." Authority was also given to cut down the ailanthus tree at the back of the building.[107]

York's plan led to replacement of the plain four-pane front windows with diamond-patterned glass, evoking a colonial or Tudor mode. The front door, formerly a double panel, was replaced by a single with two glass panels in metalwork. Recent expert inspection has shown that partitions were removed on the first floor. The trap door into the second floor was replaced by an open entry at the top of the stairs. A small toilet linked to a sewer line was placed on the second floor. The walls were plastered near the end of 1926. In the spring of 1927 a fireplace was built at the north end of the first floor.[108]

Repair and reconstruction went on from the fall of 1926 to mid-1927. Samuel Nardone & Co., masons and contractors in Westerly, charged for materials, labor, and travel for "pointing and cutting windows": trucks, driller, masons, cement, lime, sand, hodcarriers, and daily carfare amounted to $232.05. Leon Piver* of Main Street, a mason, submitted a bill on December 29, 1926, for 135

* Leon Piver's grandson Josh, who died in the attack on the World Trade Center in 2001, has a small memorial on the lawn on the east side of the Point, not far from the Old Lighthouse Museum.

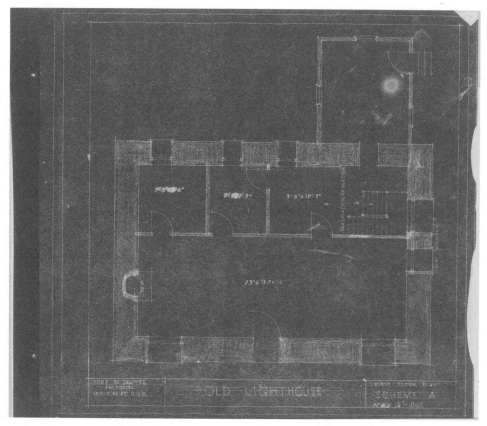

Edward Palmer York was authorized by the Historical Society governors on August 20, 1926, to proceed with his "Scheme A" in altering the Lighthouse to display the Society's collection.

hours of labor for himself, at 90 cents an hour, and 135 more for a helper at 70 cents an hour. The bill also indicates that 78 bags of plaster were used as well as three loads of gravel and other materials. The total was $339.48. The next spring, Nardone came back to deal with the fireplace. Four days of work required 400 bricks, two stone posts, other materials and twenty hours of mason's labor as well as four hours of carpentry, for a total of $235.65. On June 25, 1927, the

Society added up its bills: carpentry, $715; masons & plasterers. $571.53; wiring, $80; insurance, $30 — a total of $1,396.53, leaving a balance of $800 in the treasury.[109]

The roof remained a chronic problem, even after the museum opened. York wrote to Williams on November 27, 1928, that he had estimates for various replacement materials: $1,500 for slate; $800 for "the very heavy Johns Manville asbestos shingle," and $600 for a very heavy shaved shingle. The "ordinary shingle" he had on his house cost $400, he reported.* At a special meeting on April 13, 1929, members learned that enough money had been collected to put a new slate roof over the whole lighthouse.[110]

The Society continued to be preoccupied as well by a distraction that had arrived with the original purchase: The government still owned the strip of land along Water Street used for a Weather Bureau signal mast constructed in 1917. The Society began to fear that "strangers" might buy the Weather Bureau easement and seal the future museum off from visitors entering from Water Street. On June 28, 1926, the Society president wrote to the Bureau of Lighthouses asking to buy the strip. The Society also asked for help from Representative Freeman. In mid-July, the Bureau of Lighthouses replied that the Weather Bureau strip was not to be part of any sale so long as the government needed the signal tower. By 1935 the weather tower was gone and the site was used as Society property, although efforts as recently as 2013 to ascertain its ownership indicate that the federal government never formally yielded the strip.[111]

However, the Society failed to foresee a much bigger future problem next door. The government continued to own the 1908 keeper's dwelling, home to the employees who tended the breakwater lights. The dwelling's north wall stood only a few feet from the south wall of the lighthouse. In 1926, the government decided to close and demolish the West Breakwater Light and replaced it with an automatic device. The keeper's house was to be sold to the highest bidder.

* That was the end of York's services to the Society; he died unexpectedly at the end of 1928. He was remembered as an architect of large buildings; the lighthouse certainly must have been among the smallest of his projects. See obituary in the *New York Times,* December 31, 1928.

Photograph taken in the late 1920s shows both the lighthouse tower and the Weather Bureau storm-warning tower just beyond. Observer is young Shep Smith, whose family lived in the old keeper's house. If all three lamps on the tower are lit (two reds with a white in the middle) winds of sixty-four knots are expected. *(Courtesy of Henry Robinson Palmer III)*

The new windows with diamond-shaped panes selected by Edward Palmer York show in this professional photograph. It was taken in the nineteen-twenties, judging by the clothes of the women on the front steps. *(Courtesy of Henry Robinson Palmer III)*

Even while rejecting the Society's offer to buy the Weather Bureau strip, acting commissioner Conway said that the Society could bid on the keeper's house. There was no response by the Society.[112]

On September 27, 1926, the keeper's house and lot, totaling about half an acre, were sold to Wilson Fitch Smith, a civil engineer from New York, for $5,610, almost $2,000 more than the lighthouse. For forty years, the house remained more or less at the same scale on which it had been built. But a sequence of owners in the late twentieth century expanded the footprint, all but dwarfing the old lighthouse and blocking it from Stonington Point. In recent years, the expansion of what had come to be called the Point House has produced a structure of nearly 6,000 square feet, almost four times the size of the lighthouse, which was destined to spent much of each day in its shadow. The Society's later leaders might well have wished that their predecessors had worried about the keeper's dwelling rather than the tiny Weather Bureau strip.[113]

The Society decided to open its new museum in 1927. At its meeting on June 25, the board named a committee of three women – Mrs. Edward Palmer York, Mrs. F. R. Carrington and Mrs. Walter Cole — to "attend immediately to the interior painting etc. so that the house might be ready for the collecting and placing of the exhibit." This exhibit, later records indicate, probably included a lot of printed matter, some silverware, china, pottery, firearms, 1814 cannonballs, yarn winders, spinning wheels: a display of materials ranging from great value to possibly none. The 1814 battle flag was not on display.[114]

On August 10, 1927, the 113th anniversary of the Battle of Stonington, the Old Lighthouse Museum was opened to the public. The Society created a looseleaf register for visitors and on opening day 153 signed in, among them the long-time Borough warden (mayor) Cornelius B. Crandall and many of the officers of the Society. Admission was free and remained so for more than a decade. On most days, the woman assigned to be "hostess" or "receptionist" — the on-site person for the Society — signed in first. Accounts show hostesses were sometimes paid — $72 for the summer at one point–but evidently volunteers were more common.[115]

On July 14, 1928, the Historical Society hired the person who probably still holds the record for the longest tenure as its employee: Joseph Santos, the caretaker for the Lighthouse. Santos held the post for over fifty years, until November 1978, when health forced him to yield the job. Santos, born on Saõ Miguel in the Azores on September 15, 1905, emigrated to the United States at 15. On the job in a Fall River weaver's shop, he met Mary Pimentel, and they married. Because Mary had a sister working in the Velvet Mill, the couple moved in 1928 to Stonington, where Santos also worked in the mill. They lived on Omega Street and the family soon became involved with the Lighthouse next door, he as caretaker and handyman and his wife, after a time, as a gardener. George Lothrop Campbell, director of the Lighthouse in 1979, wrote then that Santos was "far more than a caretaker." Campbell added: "He kept up the

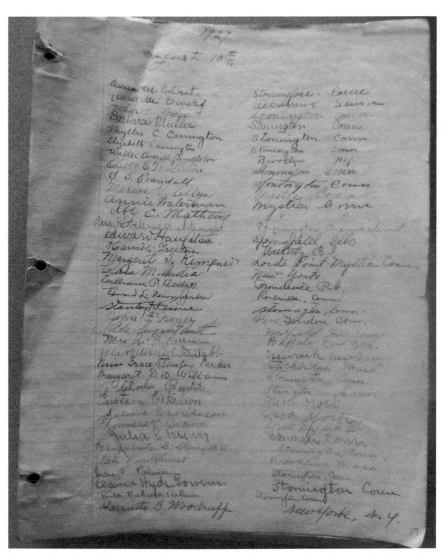

On August 10, 1927, the 113th anniversary of the Battle of Stonington, the Historical Society opened its new museum in the Lighthouse. Admission was free. The Society created a looseleaf register for visitors and 153 signed in, including Cornelius B. Crandall, the long-time Warden of Stonington Borough, and many officers of the Society.

building, always solving a battery of problems . . . and doing so with perceptive resourcefulness."

The Santos family moved from Omega Street, and for a time lived in the Arcade on Water Street, where they ran a candy store, May's Variety Shop. When the Lighthouse mounted an exhibition about the Portuguese heritage in Stonington, the Santoses gave as a gift a specially made Portuguese flag. Their son Raymond dealt with the Lighthouse grounds and their grandson David, who worked with his grandfather, was chosen by the Society to take the job when Joseph could not continue. The Society honored Joseph's long service in his last active summer, and he died on March 1, 1979.[116]

In 1932, the site of the first lighthouse, closed ninety-two years before, reverted at last to Stonington Borough. On June 26, 1932, 0.48 acres identified as "Stonington Point" were conveyed by the federal secretary of commerce. The conveyance said the gift was "for improvement and maintenance as a plaza in commemoration of those valiant men who so nobly defended it during the three-day bombardment by the British fleet under Commodore Hardy on August 9, 10 and 11, 1814." The tract, now mostly a parking lot, had remained in government hands for 109 years.[117]

Joseph Santos (1908-1979) was caretaker of the Lighthouse for fifty years, 1928 to 1978. He and his wife, Mary Pimentel, had a Portuguese flag made for a Historical Society exhibition about the Portuguese influence in Stonington. They were honored by the Society in 1978. *(Historical Footnotes, photo by Charles Thibeault)*

These four photographs, from the west, south, north, and east sides of the Lighthouse, were tracked down, with the help of Wick York, grandson of Edward Palmer York, in the still pictures reference department of the National Archives. The documentation says the photos were sent to the government in 1929 by T.W. Cutler of the Stonington Historical Society. Cutler, the registrar of the Society, was in charge of its collections. It seems most likely that the photographs were made close to 1925, when the Lighthouse was bought by the Historical Society. The curling newspaper pasted in the windows demonstrates that the Lighthouse is not inhabited. The holes through the original photos are not explained.

Stonington Lighthouse

Stonington Historical Society

Admission Free

Tea Daily Except Monday

SIXTY CENTS

LUNCHEON AND DINNER SERVED ON ORDER

Tel. Mystic 395J3

Mrs. Sims Stillman

The Tearoom Years

The serving of tea was an idea that had hung around ever since Anne Atwood Dodge had mentioned it before the Society bought the lighthouse. Since there was no admission charge or other revenue, the officers decided to open a tearoom in the museum's first year. Mrs. Edward Palmer York, wife of the Society's architectural adviser and one of the committee that prepared the lighthouse for its opening, advanced $160 to create a terrace on the east side of the building. In the brief 1927 tearoom season, the net was $176.85. A yearly concession arrangement was made with a caterer to serve tea and sometimes other meals on a terrace and in front of the lighthouse, where umbrellas and tables were set up. The Society got a negotiated percentage of the yield, which never reached four figures.[118]

The operation of the lighthouse and tearoom remained more or less the same until World War II. The concession agreement for summer 1941 depicts the tearoom operation in its maturity. The concessionaire was Mrs. Sims Stillman of New York City and Florida. It reveals, among other things, that the lighthouse was serving as a dormitory: "You will have the same privilege as last year to live in the Lighthouse without payment of rent." Her assistant's room, also presumably in the lighthouse, was charged to Mrs. Stillman's account at $5 a week. Her responsibilities were the costs of food, electricity, gas, helpers, toll calls, and laundry. William Rose, a worker at the lighthouse, would carry the garbage to the street and set out the chairs, umbrellas, and large tables. "Any other services required of Mr. Rose will be paid by you." This agreement was sent by J. Culbert Palmer on his legal letterhead from 60 Broadway, New York, to Mrs. Sims at her home on West 55th Street, New York.

Facing page: An advertising card for tea at the Lighthouse was printed in 1940 or 1941. Daily tea was sold for sixty cents, and admission to the Lighthouse—not described here as a museum—was free.

The year the Historical Society opened the Lighthouse to the public, 1927, it hired a concessionaire to serve tea there. This photograph was taken before September 1938, when the terrace, created for tearoom use east of the building, was destroyed in the hurricane.

It appeared that the tearoom operation had largely overshadowed attention to the lighthouse as a museum. The Society's collection came in for glancing consideration at a meeting on July 24, 1936. A plea was made for "loans or gifts which would better the standard of the exhibition." By June 1938, the collection got some attention. The annual meeting heard of a visit from a Works Progress Administration textiles expert who was working on the Index of American Design. He wanted to photograph two "valuable pieces" of crewel work in the collection and would provide a free copy of each photo for the Society. Later in the same meeting: "The recording secretary was authorized to make inquiries as how best to preserve the old flag. There was a possibility of receiving government aid to do so. It was moved, seconded and voted that the Society accept no government aid for the purpose."[119]

This sign, one of several like it that survive, points to the difficulty the Historical Society experienced in changing the Lighthouse grounds from an open field around a derelict building to a site for tea and conversation.

The Connecticut volume of the American Guide Series, written under the aegis of the Federal Writers Project, was published in 1938. It devoted six and a half pages to a tour of Stonington. "The Old Stone Lighthouse," — "now a museum and tearoom" — got three paragraphs, one devoted to the Boston-built barque *Great Republic,* because the museum at that time had on loan the ship's massive eagle figurehead, which had been acquired by Captain Nathaniel B. Palmer. The figurehead was later transferred and sold to Mystic Seaport. The remainder of the collection got this appraisal: "Other exhibits include a Liverpool pitcher made in celebration of 'The Gallant Defense of Stonington,' several pieces of old pewter, spinning and weaving implements and equipment, nautical instruments, old books, bank notes, bedspreads, fabrics, portraits, and documents."[120]

Stonington Borough lay in the path of the memorable hurricane of 1938. Stonington's fishing fleet was all but destroyed, as were dozens of buildings and hundreds of trees. However, the lighthouse escaped with minor damage.

Margaret Williams, the recording secretary, wrote the following directly into the bound pages of the minutes book:

> The hurricane of September 21, 1938, did considerable damage to the grounds and building of the Stonington Historical Society. The shore line on the East side of the property was washed back 25 to 30 feet and a sewer line damaged; the trees around the Terrace were killed and also many of the bushes along the north line. The north-east corner of the roof was entirely lost; and trucks, ladders etc. used in repairing it completed the ruin of the Terrace.

Eugene Atwood II, the treasurer in 1939, reported that repairs after the storm came to $755.88: $623.18 for work on the building itself, $79.25 for the grounds, and $53.45 for the sewage system.[121]

The lighthouse remained open in 1942, the first year of American participation in World War II, until Labor Day. It was in the care of Portia LeBrun of New York, a poet and designer and friend of the artist Guy Pène Dubois, who ran an art school in Stonington during the war and painted her portrait about this time. The building was not opened to the public at all in 1943, 1944, or 1945.[122]

On July 17, 1946, the lighthouse reopened. Many names from the neighborhood, particularly those of schoolchildren, show up on the register. The next year, on May 9, 1947, the officers, trustees and committee chairs met and decided to do nothing about repairing the lighthouse until the price of materials, inflated at the end of the war, dropped again. The lighthouse was opened on June 25, but the tearoom was "poorly patronized." On June 8, 1948, it was reported that the incumbent concessionaire could not do the teas that summer, and it was too late to find a replacement; the lighthouse did not open that year.[123]

CREATING A MUSEUM

The 1948 closing may have been a low point, but rescue was ahead. For one thing, in 1947 the Society elected a vigorous new president, Griffith Baily Coale, famed not only for his work as a muralist but for his dramatic paintings of naval combat during World War II. Moreover, on December 16, 1948, the minutes describe the advent of two former New Yorkers who were destined to rescue the lighthouse and its collection: Stephen Hurlbut and his wife, Irene Turnure. A subsequent curator, George Campbell, said that the Hurlbuts saved the museum from "confusion," but their work did a great deal more. A decade of effort by these two, initially propelled by Coale, opened the way to the Stonington Historical Society's growth into a serious educational institution and established the Old Lighthouse with standing as a small but valuable museum.[124]

Hurlbut, a dealer in colonial antiques, had a business that was affiliated with a London firm but whose company failed in the Depression. Mrs. Hurlbut was an interior decorator who operated the Tower Shop in New York. They sold their country place in New Jersey in 1947 and shifted to Stonington, where they bought a collapsing historic house. Money was not a problem but they were in quest of something to do with their lives.[125]

Their stewardship at the Historical Society began one rainy afternoon in the fall of 1948, as Hurlbut wrote in a report a decade later. Coale, he said, "lured us down to take a serious look at the Lighthouse and its collection." Hurlbut recalled:

> The whole town was beginning to prepare for the coming Tricentennial, and [Coale was] well aware that the Lighthouse and its contents were due for a thorough refurbishing. The building had been closed during the

Griffith Baily Coale (1890-1950), a muralist and World War II Navy combat painter, was elected president of the Historical Society in 1947. As a Navy lieutenant commander, Coale was in an Atlantic convoy when the *U.S.S. Reuben James* was sunk by the Germans in October 1941; it was the first U.S. vessel lost to enemy action in World War II. His depiction showed sailors dying in the sea below him as the ship disappeared. The painting, exhibited by the New-York Historical Society in 2013, remains vivid and terrifying after seventy-two years.

Elsa Hurlbut, later Elsa H. Cole, on the left, her father, Stephen Hurlbut, and her mother, Irene Turnure Hurlbut, in Stonington in the late nineteen-forties. *(Courtesy of Elsa Hurlbut Cole)*

War, and before then had been less a museum than an attractive tea room with historical exhibits on the side. By 1948 it was clear that the day of tea rooms was over, and what the Society really needed was a genuine and interesting little regional museum which could stand on its own feet, and contribute something to the life of the community beyond being merely a repository for local relics.

We were so struck by the opportunity to do something interesting and creative, using the modern techniques which have revolutionized small museums throughout the country, that we fell at once into Grif's trap, and volunteered to do the job.

That December, the Hurlbuts reported to a Society meeting that "silverfish had eaten many of the exhibits, especially the Battle Flag of 1812 and the ink off the labels." They requested permission to hire a janitor to keep the stove in the lighthouse going so they could work all winter.[126]

In the winter of 1948-49, they sorted, inventoried, obtained new display cases, installed floodlighting, planned and painted. They uncovered objects given to the Society that had never been displayed — for example, a "linsey-woolsey covered wooden saddle tucked away under the eaves." To evaluate this one, they got help from a curator at Colonial Williamsburg. The famous flag they found "folded up in a showcase, in a very sad state of repair." The Hurlbuts' work of salvage was informed not only by their previous careers but by outside research. Elsa H. Cole, their daughter, said that her parents jaunted off that winter to Wisconsin and Minnesota to look at small museums and learn about their collections and operations. By virtue of this exertion, they became the first people with curatorial skills to contribute work to the Society.[127]

After the winter's work, the Board met on March 8, 1949. Coale was in full battle mode to save the museum, with the help of the Hurlbuts. He convened the officers at his home on Water Street. The minutes read:

Coale explained that the time had come when money must be spent to preserve the collection. The collection was virtually uncatalogued and had been allowed to go to rot from lack of care. It should be cleaned at least once a year and moth balls put in whenever necessary. The Society's stewardship of gifts and loans has been awful disgraceful. . . .

The Hurlbuts reported that the papers had been sorted previously, (by

Dr. and Mrs. Williams and Miss Louise Trumbull). It was planned to move the papers, books and textiles to the Bank Building when there was adequate heat, light etc. to make them accessible to the public throughout the year. The textiles were in terrible condition–moth-eaten and rotten. He [Coale] read excerpts from his correspondence with Admiral Richey on the flag. There are few flags left from the War of 1812. This one is 11 ¼ by 18 and has 17 stars and 17 stripes [actually, 16 of each], evidently unique. The flag could be backed so it could be hung against a wall. At present the flag was in the wine vault of the New York Yacht Club. It would cost $1,000 to have it preserved.

Coale, backed by the Hurlbuts' testimony, raised the money to send the flag off to Brooklyn, New York, to the atelier of Katherine Fowler Richey and her husband, Admiral Thomas Richey. The couple had worked with Mrs. Richey's mother, Amelia Fowler, supervisor of the 1914 restoration of the Star Spangled Banner. After being stitched to a backing, this premier possession was installed in the bank building on Cannon Square that the Society had acquired in 1940, behind glass, in time for the tricentennial of the town in July 1949. It remained in the Ocean Bank building until January 2004.[128]

The Coale-Hurlbut alliance came to an end in August 1950, when Coale died. The annual meeting was held a few weeks later at the Lighthouse for the first time. Hurlbut was elected to succeed Coale but his report was submitted in the third person for himself and his wife as curators. It clearly shows what a transformation had been achieved in only two years. The lighthouse was having its second successful season, he said, "standing on its own feet strictly as a museum, without a tea room as an added attraction." He added that there had already been almost a thousand-admission paying visitors in two months.

Hurlbut remained as president for nine years. While still refurbishing the interior of the lighthouse, he also dealt with damage to the site from Hurricane Carol in 1954. The Society had to allocate $4,000 to build a seawall on the Little Narragansett Bay, or eastern, side. It was completed in 1956 and still stands.[129]

Hurlbut prefaced his final report, dated February 5, 1958, this way:

> Before proceeding to the election of trustees, I think it is in order for me to submit, for the record, a rather personal farewell report. I know that I would have been glad to see anything of the sort left by my predecessors

in office. Their objectives were no doubt all basically the same as ours, but it would be interesting to know how they thought these should be approached.

I have been President for nearly nine years, with Mrs. Hurlbut as Curator doing most of the really hard work — planning the reorganization of the Museum in the first place, staging special summer exhibitions, putting the Lighthouse to bed every fall and waking it up against every spring, keeping her eye on the custodians and helping me every inch of the way . . .

Stephen Hurlbut died suddenly on June 1, 1960. In his honor a plaque was placed in the museum, with a text created by his friend, the critic John Mason Brown, a Stonington summer resident, who was related to Irene Hurlbut's daughters by her first marriage:

> In grateful memory of Stephen Hurlbut
> President of the Historical Society 1948-1957
> A lean, tall man wide in his interests
> Large in his imagination and
> Impeccable in his tastes,
> Who with his wife, Irene,
> Brought light again to this Lighthouse
> By recognizing that foregrounds are
> Impossible without backgrounds, and by
> Keeping alive Stonington's proud past.[130]

The leadership of the Hurlbuts raised the status of the lighthouse from that of a tearoom with historical souvenirs to a museum with a collection and curators — and a previously untapped appeal to visitors from near and far. But was it truly a *lighthouse* museum or a museum of local antiquities that happen to reside in a lighthouse? The United States Lighthouse Society, an educational organization that studies lighthouses, defines a lighthouse museum as an institution that seeks to reflect its history as a lighthouse, and Stonington's Old Lighthouse Museum never sought to meet that standard.

Age of Expansion

While the Hurlbuts put the Old Lighthouse Museum on the way to viability, the Society as a whole remained a poor relative in a village increasingly peopled by the well-off. During his tenure, Hurlbut remarked that the organization had only "a few hundred dollars in the bank, plus an endowment of some two thousand dollars, and our income was negligible." Nonetheless, the Society accepted several opportunities to acquire new properties.

In 1940, the 1851 Ocean Bank building facing Cannon Square in the Borough was offered for sale, its previous occupant having failed. Williams Haynes, a journalist and historian of the chemical industry who had moved to Stonington in the 1930s, drafted an ambitious plan that included purchase of the bank building by the Society and its use as the Society's headquarters and as a second museum. The Society purchased the bank building in 1942 for $2,000. With the United States now engaged in war, the Society deferred its grand plan and leased the building to the American Red Cross "until ninety days after the cessation of hostilities," an agreement that was extended several times.[131]

Ten years later, the Society also acquired the Arcade, given to the Society in 1951 as a gift from Frederic C. Horner. Just north of the Ocean Bank building on Water Street in the Borough, the Arcade was a colonnaded wooden structure built after the 1837 Borough fire. It had rentable spaces for shops or, later, apartments or offices, which the Society leased. Meanwhile the Society had given up the idea of using the bank building as its own headquarters and rented it to the New London City National Bank, the first in a long series of banks to operate branches there. Together the modest rental income from the two buildings helped keep the Society afloat in lean years and also met the standard enunciated by the architecture critic Ada Louise Huxtable — preservation through use.[132]

A third acquisition did not turn out so well. In 1962, the Society was offered a colonial house on Route 27 in Mystic known as Whitehall Mansion. It stood on the right-of-way for the new Interstate 95, and thus had to be moved or demolished. It was offered to the Historical Society by its owners with a piece of land to which it could be moved. In the debate over whether to accept the gift, Hurlbut's successor as president, Stuart Webb, resigned. Irene Hurlbut succeeded him temporarily and the Society accepted Whitehall.

A new president elected in 1964, Captain Robert J. Ramsbotham, a retired naval officer, destined to serve for twenty-five years, undertook the task of preparing Whitehall for use. In acquiring the property, the Society shifted its focus from Stonington's maritime roots — and farther from the Old Lighthouse Museum — to the kind of old-colonial-house headquarters often favored by New England historical societies. Whitehall was given top priority in the Society's fundraising and publicity (notably in its new newsletter, *Historical Footnotes*) and when it opened in 1969 it became the Society's headquarters, meeting place, and library. It also offered several rooms of conventional colonial objects. But in the long run Whitehall did not work, financially or organizationally: It proved too distant for most members, and researchers found access to the library difficult. Moreover, it utterly lacked the salt-air flavor that permeated Stonington's history. It was sold in the mid-1990s, was moved again, and became part of a motel property.[133]

Meanwhile, the Hurlbut influence at the lighthouse continued for a time with the efforts of Irene Hurlbut, assisted later by Emily Lynch, who took charge of educational programs and founded the Society's education committee, and Lydia Bond Powel, keeper emeritus of the American Wing at the Metropolitan Museum of Art. In 1968, Mrs. Powel became chair of the Society's museum committee and compiled a professional assessment of the condition and prospects of the lighthouse. Her critique enumerated evident shortcomings in the preservation and security of the collections. Moreover, she focused attention on the woebegone lighthouse structure itself, saturated with moisture, afflicted with mold, an imperfect vessel for a museum.

Portrait of "King" David Chesebrough (1702/3-1782) was a pivotal part of the collection in the Lighthouse. It was sold in a time of straitened finances and then repurchased. *(Photograph by Mary Beth Baker)*

She found, however, that the Society, having concentrated its resources on establishing Whitehall, could not mount a second fundraising campaign, nor did she, now elderly, wish to lead such an effort. As a stopgap, she recommended sale of three of the lighthouse collection's most valuable paintings, all from the colonial era and associated with the founding Chesebrough family.[134]

The Vose Gallery in Boston bought outright a 1732 portrait of "King" David Chesebrough, great-grandson of the Stonington founding father William Chesebrough, and accepted portraits of his daughter and son-in-law on consignment. The two other pictures show Abigail, daughter of David, painted by Joseph Blackburn, and Abigail's husband, Alexander Grant, painted by Cosmo Alexander.

The price for the David Chesebrough picture in 1969 was $17,500. The painting of David Chesebrough was the work of John Smibert, a leading portrait painter of New England's colonial elite, and was at the time by far the most valuable of the three. How these three paintings came to be the property of the Stonington Historical Society would be funny if it were not so nearly a major loss for the organization.

In the early years of the twentieth century, Bessie Williams Sherman of Chicago became the surviving direct heir of David Chesebrough. Her will left the paintings to the Stonington Historical Society. In 1915, after her death, her executors crated the three paintings and sent them by rail C.O.D. to Stonington, with a note that the Historical Society would pay the freight. The society, clearly unaware what was at stake, refused to pay the bill and the paintings were stashed in the loft of a coal shed near the depot.

Eight years later, in 1923, the Society put out a plea for old portraits of local interest for an exhibition. Dr. Charles M. Williams, a cousin of the late Mrs. Sherman, remembered something about her bequest. A search was made through the town and the portraits were found, still in their crates. The fees were presumably paid and the paintings created a stir at the exhibition.

In 1970, Powel asked George Campbell to succeed her as chair of the lighthouse committee. Campbell, a teacher in local private schools, had become widely involved in nonprofit volunteer work since coming to Stonington, and

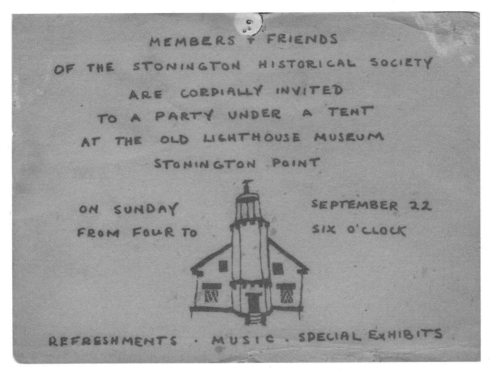

MEMBERS + FRIENDS
OF THE STONINGTON HISTORICAL SOCIETY
ARE CORDIALLY INVITED
TO A PARTY UNDER A TENT
AT THE OLD LIGHTHOUSE MUSEUM
STONINGTON POINT

ON SUNDAY
FROM FOUR TO

SEPTEMBER 22
SIX O'CLOCK

REFRESHMENTS · MUSIC · SPECIAL EXHIBITS

This postcard invitation to the Historical Society's annual meeting September 22, 1974, uses the engaging drawing made by Sibby Lynch when she was working at the Lighthouse while in school. Ms. Lynch also designed the sign that hung outside the gate.

he threw himself wholeheartedly into the work of managing the lighthouse, a task he carried on for more than twenty years. His first order of business was to complete the transactions Mrs. Powel had begun. At length the paintings of the Cheserough daughter and son-in-law were sold, and Campbell used part of the proceeds to repurchase the valuable David Chesebrough portrait from the gallery where it had been awaiting a buyer. It has remained in the collection since.[135]

But Campbell, like Powel, found that the most critical issue was the condition of the building, now 130 years old. He recalled later: "The two foot thick stone

Stefan Celichowski (center), head of the Lighthouse Committee of the Historical Society board in the 1990s, in the Lighthouse yard with his hands-on garden work group.

walls of the unheated 1840 structure, so close to the sound and exposed to the elements, were largely saturated with moisture. In fact, water was oozing through a number of places. . . . The trapped humidity made for the worst possible environment for a museum."

With the help of John Lincoln, local architect and son-in-law of Edward Palmer York, leakage along the east wall was eased and wood that had been attacked by rot and vermin was braced. Hot air heating was installed in 1971, mostly to dry the environment, and a security system eventually guarded against the thefts that had afflicted the museum since the late 1960s. An infestation of powder post beetles required fumigation in 1972. But the building, like an incurable and aging patient, seemed never to enjoy good health, and many others ministered to it as the decades went by.[136]

When Campbell left the post of the lighthouse committee chair in 1990, a member of the Society board, Stefan Celichowski, who lived on Omega Street close to the lighthouse, eventually became its manager. He became a strong advocate of needed improvements and innovations at the lighthouse. An example was the installation in 2003 of sturdy glass windows in the floor under the stairs to display the old cistern and well, giving an idea of what living in a lighthouse might have been like. The weathervane was repaired and reinstalled above the lantern. The slate roof was restored in 2009.[137]

In 1971, Louise Pittaway arrived; she is the person who became most closely linked to the lighthouse museum through the rest of the twentieth century. Pittaway, an editor of medical books, moved to Stonington when her husband went to work for Electric Boat in Groton. She took an hourly summer job at the lighthouse as the on-site expert, overseer, and trainer of volunteers. She completed her degree at Connecticut College in 1976 and that year, according to Campbell's report in *Historical Footnotes,* took charge of daily operations at the lighthouse.

In 1984, she was designated curator of the Old Lighthouse Museum, thus becoming the Historical Society's first long-term professional employee. Like Mrs. Hurlbut, she conceived of exhibitions, sought local objects, and mounted the displays: inkwell collections, kitchen tools, stone-wall photographs. In addition, Mrs. Pittaway was an editor for the Connecticut League of Historical Societies from 1984 to 1999.[138]

In more than thirty-five years of service, ending in 2010, she devoted her major efforts to expanding the visiting schedule for the lighthouse, ultimately creating a calendar so it was open every day from May 1 to October 31, while finding volunteers to cover the extended hours. Attendance continued to rise: 3,000 visitors in 1971, doubling previous years; 5,000 in 1982; nearly 8,000 in 1986, and nearly 10,000 in 1987.

The lighthouse historian Jeremy D'Entremont observed: "There's no other lighthouse on the Connecticut coast that's open as often." Mrs. Pittaway commented: "It pleases me that our lighthouse has been a leader in welcoming visitors inside and allowing them access to the tower, unlike so many that can only be viewed from the grounds. I think townspeople are proud of our lighthouse and its fine museum and think of it as an important local point of interest."[139]

Mrs. Pittaway died at 77 in May 2013.

Louise Pittaway, who started as a summer volunteer in 1975 and served as curator of the Lighthouse from 1984 to 2010, stands at the tower doorway of the Lighthouse.

Display on second floor of the Lighthouse with a map showing placement of lights on Long Island Sound, and a fourth-order Fresnel lens, lent by the Coast Guard. In 1856, when the Stonington Lighthouse was operating, it received a Fresnel lens of the sixth order, seventeen inches high, the smallest made. It was the standard for lights in harbors. Mary di Cecco, long-time assistant curator, is demonstrating the interactive map.

At the end of 1994, the Historical Society, under the presidency of Dr. Norman F. Boas, swung its center of gravity yet again: to the house known as Pine Point or the Palmer-Loper House, once home to Stonington's most famous skipper, Captain Nathaniel Brown Palmer, and his brother, Alexander, lying just north of Stonington Borough. Purchase of the house, built in the 1850s, was financed partly through the sale of Whitehall, and with the aid of state funds and a gift from Marcia Woolworth Porter in memory of her late husband, Richard W. Woolworth. With part of this gift and a major capital campaign, the Society built the modern climate-controlled Richard W. Woolworth Library and Research Center on land adjoining the Palmer House. Many of the Society's vulnerable artifacts were moved to this sanctuary away from the damp light-house.[140]

The Lighthouse Endures

As the twenty-first century began, the 1840 Lighthouse maintained its position as Society's — and Stonington Borough's — most popular site for visitors. While its collections continued to be an interesting patchwork, its curious entrance, its tower, lantern space, cistern and well, its massive walls, its rolling grounds and seawall, all displayed in the embrace of the Atlantic, drew children and adults, and all who loved lighthouses, week after week and summer after summer.

By 2012, it was clear, however, that the Lighthouse required serious work. It still leaked. It needed an up-to-date introduction for visitors unfamiliar with the purpose and development of lighthouses. It required access for those who cannot get up steps. So once again the Society's leaders called in experts to see how best to protect the piece of history it bought from the Government and turned into a museum.

In 1975, the Old Lighthouse Museum was nominated for the National Register of Historic Places and was accepted January 1, 1976. Commenting on its enduring value, the nominator, Bruce Clouette of the Connecticut Historical Commission, took a particular view of the value of the lighthouse:

> The Stonington Harbor Lighthouse is a significant historic property because it typifies the history of American lighthouse policy and because it is an essential element in the physical preservation of Stonington's maritime heritage. Because it served as a sentinel for Stonington Harbor,

the lighthouse is important in preserving the town's past. The major activities in 19th century Stonington were shipbuilding and refitting whaling and sealing vessels. These produced a large amount of commercial activity, and hence the life of the town depended on the harbor. The significance of the lighthouse is increased by its location at the southern end of Stonington Borough, an area rich in 18th and 19th century buildings. Finally, in its fortress-like construction and detailing, unusual for a lighthouse, and its thematic unity — solidness, as befits its function — the Stonington Harbor Lighthouse is an architectural resource.[141]

This assessment might well serve as a continuing reminder of the inadequacy of the persistent idea that the lighthouse is valuable only as a space for displaying artifacts and storing miscellany. Instead, as Clouette insisted, the lighthouse is a symbol and a tangible representation of Stonington's maritime past, but has not yet fulfilled its historical possibilities.

APPENDIX

This essay was written by Stephen Hurlbut for the annual meeting of 1958, when he was stepping down from the Society's presidency. His report covers a time, crucial to the Old Lighthouse Museum and to the Society itself, of almost a decade when the Hurlbuts shut the door on the Lighthouse as a tearoom and reopened it as a place where local history and artifacts could be examined and researched, and adults and children could come to learn. Half a century later, this report, reprinted here in its entirety, offers not just the first-person narrative of a couple who did "something interesting and creative," but a lucid statement of problems still faced by the Society, of goals and ideas that give valid direction.

STONINGTON HISTORICAL SOCIETY
President's Report to Annual Meeting
February 5, 1958

Final report of Stephen Hurlbut showing the progress of Stonington Historical Society during the nine years of his Presidency.

Before proceeding to the election of trustees, I think it is in order for me to submit, for the record, a rather personal farewell report. I know I would have been glad to see anything of the sort left by my predecessors in office. Their objectives were no doubt all basically the same as ours, but it would be interesting to know how they thought these had best be approached.

I have been President for nearly nine years, with Mrs. Hurlbut as Curator doing most of the really hard work — planning the reorganization of the Museum in the first place, staging special summer exhibitions, putting the Lighthouse to bed every fall and waking it up again every spring, keeping her eye on the custodians and helping me every inch of the way in our reconstruction of the Arcade. Our connection with the Society began back in the fall of 1948, when one rainy afternoon Griffith Coale, then President, lured us down to take a serious look at the Lighthouse and its collection. The whole town was beginning to prepare for the coming Tricentennial, and he was well aware that the Lighthouse and its contents were due for a thorough refurbishing. The building had been closed during the War, and before then had been less a museum than an attractive tea room with historical exhibits on the side. By 1948 it was clear that the day of tea rooms was over, and that what Stonington really needed was a genuine and interesting little regional museum which could stand on its own feet, and contribute something to the life of the community beyond being merely a repository for local relics. We were so struck by the opportunity to do something interesting and creative, using the modern techniques which have revolutionized small museums throughout the country, that we fell at once into Grif's trap, and volunteered to do the job.

And it was a job — though definitely fun. We worked all through that winter, sorting, inventorying, having new cases made, installing flood lighting, planning and painting. The historical collection, the nucleus of which had been formed in 1914, for the Centennial of the Battle of Stonington, contained much more of interest and value than had at first been apparent, and we discovered totally unexpected treasures, like the early linsey-woolsey covered wooden saddle tucked away under the eaves, source unknown and never exhibited, which the Curator of such things at Williamsburg told us it was the only simple 18th Century sidesaddle preserved in any museum, so far as he knew. He took it to Williamsburg for the winter, where it was photographed, measured and repaired. The famous 16-stars-and-stripes Stonington Battle Flag, which we found folded up in a show case, in a very sad state of repair, was saved and restored through Grif Coale's moving appeal for special contributions to meet the cost — a thousand dollars.

We had taken on this project as a temporary job, but by the end of the successful Tricentennial summer of 1949, with its thousands of Lighthouse visitors, we could not seem to escape being elected to office. I don't believe we really minded. Well, in the course of the eight years since, our Society has not done so badly. The Museum *has* stood on its own feet — we have averaged nearly a thousand admission-paying visitors in the two summer months we are open, with a paid custodian instead of volunteer hostesses. Our permanent collection has grown slowly but steadily. We have had well over a hundred acquisitions since 1948, probably the most valuable being the extraordinary carved and painted stern board of Charles P. Williams' Stonington whaler *Mary and Susan*, bequeathed to the Society by Philip Sawyer. Just in the past few months we have had two interesting and valuable gifts, which I have brought this afternoon to demonstrate at least one of our legitimate reasons for existence.

This Swan and States jug, given us by Mrs. David Gill of Old Mystic, is the handsomest product of Stonington's early 19th Century pottery I have ever seen. Why should an industry, and a talent, which could turn out anything as perfect as this have vanished so completely? Yet no one has found even a contemporary record of this pottery. It is known that it was at the east end of Wall Street — exactly when and for how long is a mystery.

The second exhibit I have here is a diary William Chesebrough of Anguilla kept from 1773 to 1835, given us by his great-great-granddaughter, Mrs. George Lautenslager of St. Paul, Minnesota, who has also given us a bound typescript copy, an amazing job of deciphering, editing, indexing, and typing. Like most early diaries which have survived — the famous Hempstead diary the New London Historical Society published in 1901 is another local example — its preoccupation with the weather and the vital statistics of farm animals makes it pretty heavy reading. However, it covers a remarkable period of time, 62 consecutive years, and the very rarity of comments of general interest — he does pay some attention to the Battle of Stonington, and even more to the 1815 hurricane — reflects a way of life apparently so unchanging, so settled, so utterly untouched by the world at large, it is hard to realize that only a hundred years before he was born his adventurous great-great-grandfather came from England to be Stonington's first settler and that the house in which he lived most of his life would a century later be owned by immigrants from New York, the complexity of whose life would have seemed to him beyond comprehension, as indeed it sometimes does to the immigrants.

I am delighted to be able to announce that we have been promised another fine acquisition. Mrs. Griffith Coale is giving us the collection of whaling implements Grif made, which with what we already have in the Museum will make an exhibit worthy of Stonington's famous industry.

Our undigested accumulation of old manuscripts, pamphlets, newspapers, account books, and old printed records of all kinds has grown prodigiously in the past few years. It is stored in the room in the basement the Library so generously lets us use — thanks largely, I think, to the good offices of our ex-Treasurer Ed King. This material is waiting to be classified, filed, and made more easily available for research — a job which we might now afford to have undertaken professionally.

You may have gathered from the Treasurer's Report that we are a thoroughly solvent institution. In 1948 we had only a few hundred dollars in the bank, plus an endowment of some two thousand dollars, and our income was negligible. It now runs between four and five thousand a year. This is due largely to our good luck as landlords — we have kept our buildings 100% rented. Of course we would not have had them to rent if it had not been for Grif Coale's and Williams Haynes' initiative in raising the funds to buy the old "Ocean Bank," just before the War, and Fred Horner's wonderful gift of the Arcade, plus the phenomenal generosity of those who contributed well over twenty thousand dollars to convert this into such attractive units.

In spite of all this good fortune, what has been accomplished in these recent years is only a small fraction of what Mrs. Hurlbut and I would have liked to do. We hoped, in the first flush of enthusiasm, to be able to interest a far larger proportion of Stoningtonians, for economic if not for esthetic reasons, in an organization dedicated to the preservation of their historic village and town, since it seems obvious (but apparently is not) that whatever helps to keep it unspoiled by modern changes encourages visitors, and tends to maintain and increase the value of property. Our faithful group of around 150 dues-paying members have given wonderfully generous financial support to every project we have undertaken, but it is certainly not a cross-section of the local population. It would be gratifying to at least double and triple this membership, but the secret of how to make a wider appeal has persistently eluded us.

For stimulating local interest in the Museum itself we have found that nothing can touch the sort of special exhibitions Mrs. Hurlbut put on for several summers. Hundreds of "home" visitors thronged in to see the old dolls, old headgear, and "prized possessions" — especially the favorite exhibit in this show, which you may remember was a two-headed kitten (stuffed). We had hoped, however, to do more than this in developing the Museum's potential educational value to the children of the village. It is really the lack of heat in the Lighthouse which has made any cooperation with the schools impractical, since when the schools are open the Lighthouse is closed, and vice-versa. In time, of course, we should install some simple form of heat for the sake of our exhibits, even if the building is opened only occasionally. Every winter, we have to send the Lyman Allyn our three most valuable portraits — the Smibert David Chesebrough (in 1948 this had been almost ruined by mildew), the Cosmo Alexander Grant, and our distinguished Abigail Chesebrough by Blackburn, The New London Museum is of course delighted to have them, and we know they are safe, but the trucking does the paintings, and particularly the extremely valuable original frames, no good whatsoever.

The Lighthouse grounds have been neglected. We spent over four thousand dollars after Carol to build a sea wall, but though we raised over a thousand dollars for one, an imaginative landscaping plan to make our portion of the Point as useful and attractive as it obviously could and should be, remains to be made and carried out. It may be this can be done through collaboration with the Village Improvement Society.

We can now afford many things for the Museum which we couldn't consider while we were paying for the Arcade reconstruction and the sea wall — some modern showcases, better lighting, perhaps some really adequate insurance of the collection, and as I have suggested, some form of heat. It would seem wise, however, to accumulate at the same time a substantial reserve fund, to take care of future depreciation of our buildings, and above all to be able to take quick advantage of any opportunity which may arise, as it might at any time, to buy historical property that would otherwise be lost.

Your Constitution states the objects of the Society to be "to encourage interest in and knowledge of the history of Stonington Township, and to preserve the relics and records of the past and present." It seems to me we have done well to extend the definition of relics to include buildings. In fact, I am sure we are all agreed that the Society can have no more valuable function than to help in salvaging whatever is worth salvaging of early Stonington, be it buildings or open spaces which should remain open, and that while retaining its own identity, it should co-operate with other groups which have, if only indirectly, the same objectives. I think your Society, though organized over sixty years ago, has really just begun to grow, and that it may accomplish great things in the coming years. In any event, I am very happy to be able to step out of office with the feeling that the new officers will be faced with opportunities rather than with problems.

Acknowledgments

This history was the work of many hands. We are indebted, first of all, to the National Archives in Washington and Waltham, Massachusetts, and to our guide through the morass of government records, J. Candace Clifford, who with her mother, Mary Louise Clifford, has done much to shape the history of American lighthouses. Our thanks also to the willing and skillful staff of the Archives. Wayne Wheeler, president of the United States Lighthouse Association and a historian of the development of American lighthouses, provided valuable guidance in helping us fit our Old Lighthouse Museum into the continuing history of lighthouse museums.

We also benefited from the generous help of the staff of the Stonington Historical Society, in particular the Society's executive director, Mary Beth Baker, who contributed original research on the keepers of the Stonington lighthouses and their families, provided invaluable criticism of the manuscript, and created or guided our way to many of the illustrations in this book. We also thank Elizabeth Wood, the Society's director of development, who also supplied helpful criticism and made available to us her important research on Charles Hewitt Smith, Stonington's master builder. We are indebted to Anne Thacher, director of the Society's Richard W. Woolworth Library and Research Center, for her readiness to help us ferret out the secrets of the Stonington Historical Society's records.

We owe thanks as well to the late Louise Pittaway, curator emerita of the Old Lighthouse Museum, whose interview was most helpful, and to Elsa Hurlbut Cole, daughter of Stephen and Irene Hurlbut, who played such an important part in the museum's development, and was herself a long-time trustee of the Historical Society. We appreciate the steady support of the Society's publications committee, chaired by our friend Rob Palmer (Henry Robinson Palmer III) and of the ad hoc Lighthouse Committee, chaired by David Purvis, which has been planning the future of our old lighthouse, especially Guy Hermann and Jo-Anne Cristoff of Museum Insights, initial planners of the restudy of the museum, who offered sympathetic and helpful counsel. Guy was especially helpful in tracking the ownership of the plot of land where the government weather tower stood. We thank Steven Marshall for important help in uncovering pre-museum history of the structure.

We also thank Erica Lindberg Gourd, who provided a copy of the painting of the lighthouse by her grandmother, Sara Emily Darrell, and Alisa Storrow, for providing her brother's painting of the lighthouse neighborhood and valuable photographs. Sibby Lynch Schefers dug out her original works for us to scan; thanks to her and to her mother, Emily Lynch, for endless willingness to help. Rob Palmer searched out original prints from the extensive photograph collection of his historian father, Henry Robinson Palmer Jr. Howard G. Park III enabled us to use two prints from his collection.

The Stonington Historical Society has asked us to acknowledge the funding organizations that have supported research, documentation, and planning for the Old Lighthouse Museum: the Connecticut Trust for Historic Preservation, the Community Foundation of Eastern Connecticut, and Connecticut Humanities, whose executive director, Stuart Parnes, began his distinguished career at the Old Lighthouse Museum.

Marie Carija of Mystic, who designed the five earlier books we edited for the Historical Society, has once more carried out her tasks with efficiency and grace. Our thanks to her.

James Boylan Betsy Wade

End Notes

1. Wayne Wheeler, president of the U.S. Lighthouse Society, states that he believes that Stonington's is the first old lighthouse to contain a museum. However, he adds that he does not consider Stonington's a lighthouse museum as his organization defines one because it deals only incidentally with lighthouse history. Wheeler e-mail to Betsy Wade, February 11, 2013.

2. *Annual Report of the Chief of Engineers, United States Army* (Washington: Government Printing Office, 1884), p. 630.

3. U.S. Department of Commerce, Coast and Geodetic Survey, *United States Coast Pilot: Atlantic Coast Section B, Cape Cod to Sandy Hook* (5th ed., 1950), p. 248.

4. Stonington Borough history is sketched in Henry R. Palmer, *Stonington by the Sea* (Stonington: Palmer Press, 1913). "Port of delivery": Statutes at Large, 1st Cong., 2d Sess., Chapter 35 (1790), p. 147.

5. *Connecticut Gazette*, September 30, 1800; October 6, 1801. Capt. Lawrence Furlong, *The American Coast Pilot*, 3d ed. (Newburyport: Edmund M. Blunt, 1800), pp. 69-72.

6. The standard account of the battle is James Tertius de Kay, *The Battle of Stonington: Torpedoes, Submarines, and Rockets in the War of 1812* (Annapolis: Naval Institute Press, 1990, 2013). John C. Pease and John M. Niles, *A Gazetteer of the States of Connecticut and Rhode-Island* (Hartford: William S. Marsh, 1819), p. 166.

7. Niles, *Gazetteer*, pp. 165-66. Lieutenant J. Prescott, report on Stonington harbor, December 1, 1827, H. R. Doc. 166, 25th Cong., 3d Sess, pp. 2-6. Henry R. Palmer, Jr., "The Inner Breakwater," *Historical Footnotes: Bulletin of the Stonington Historical Society*, vol. 8 (February 1971); Mary M. Thacher, "1827 Map of Stonington," *Historical Footnotes*, vol. 27 (May 1990).

8. U.S. Senate Historical Office, *The Lighthouses Act of 1789* (1991).

9. Truman R. Strobridge, *Chronology of Aids to Navigation and the Old Lighthouse Service 1716-1939* (U.S. Department of Transportation, 1980); Sarah C. Gleason, *Kindly Lights: A History of the Lighthouses of New England* (Boston: Beacon Press, 1991), pp. 27-28.

10. On Pleasonton and Winslow Lewis, see, for example, Gleason, *Kindly Lights*, pp. 39-60. Pleasonton's voluminous lighthouse correspondence is preserved in the National Archives, Record Group 26. For the text of Lewis's contract with the government of March 26, 1812, see *Compilation of Public Documents and Extracts from Reports and Papers Relating to Light-Houses, Light Vessels, and Illuminating Apparatus, and to Beacons, Buoys and Fog Signals, 1789-1871* (Washington: Government Printing Office, 1871), 4-6, hereafter referred to as *Lighthouse Papers*. Wayne Wheeler, "Winslow Lewis: A Nineteenth Century Lighthouse Scalawag," *The Keeper's Log*, summer 2005, pp. 18-24.

11. Act of May 7, 1822, 17th Cong., 1st Sess., Chapter 119. Pendleton and Denison deeds, Stonington land records, v. 17, 294-95, May 23, 1823. Stephen Pleasonton to Thomas Cushing (Collector of Customs, New London), July 11, 1822, Entry 18, vol. 6, Lighthouse Letters, RG 26, National Archives. Specifications: *Connecticut Gazette* (New London), June 23, 1823.

12. Old Field Point: Pleasonton to Richard Law, New London collector, May 31, 1823, Lighthouse Letters, 1822-1826, as cited above; see also see the Inventory of Historic Light Stations at http://www.cr.nps.gov/maritime/light/oldfield.htm. Borough 1827 map: see Prescott report, cited above. John Bishop sketch: see discussion of proposed sea wall, below. See John Warner Barber, *Connecticut Historical Collections* (1836), p. 344; online at openlibrary.org. Painting: portrait of Captain Thomas Burtch of Stonington, attributed to Orlando Hand Bears, c. 1835.

13. See list of nine bids submitted, July 21, 1823, Lighthouse Letters, 1822-1826, as cited above, and final accounting, January 24, 1824, by Richard Law, showing a payment of $2,500 to Benjamin Chace and a total cost, including his own commission of $71, of $2,916. Custom House records, National Archives, Waltham.

14. James Hammond Trumbull, comp., *The Defence of Stonington* (Hartford, 1864), pp .22-23; original document is in the files of the Woolworth Library of the Stonington Historical Society, as is Potter's honorable discharge.

15. Deserters: *Democratic Press*, New London, September 24, 1813; *Niles Weekly Register*, October 2, 1813; de Kay, *Battle of Stonington*, pp. 67-68. Fanning to Commodore Isaac Chauncey, September 23, 1823, Correspondence Relating to Early Lighthouses, 1803-1852, New London, Box 4, NC-31, Record Group 26, National Archives. Rope walk: *Canton* (Ohio) *Repository*, October 12, 1815.

16. Potter-Barker family data compiled by Mary Beth Baker from family file in Stonington Historical Society records, U.S. Census data, and *The Geer Genealogy: a Historical Record of George and Thomas Geer and Their Descendants in the United States from 1623 to 1923* (New York: Brentano's, 1923). She suggests that Potter was a sailor who had deserted from the Royal Navy, but concedes that it cannot be proved.

17. Petition dated April 23, 1822, Correspondence Relating to Early Lighthouses, 1803-1852, as cited above. Since the petition is dated before passage of the legislation approving the lighthouse, it raises a question of misdating. However, there is no doubt that the year 1822 is written clearly on the document.

18. Fanning to Commodore Isaac Chauncey, September 23, 1823, Correspondence Relating to Early Lighthouses, 1803-1852, as cited above.

19. Richard Law to Pleasonton, October 16, 1823, entry 17C, letters received from Superintendents of Lights, 1803-1852, Box 22, NC 31, RG 26, National Archives.

20. Monroe appointment: Daniel Preston, ed., *Catalogue of the Correspondence and Papers of President Monroe* (Westport: Greenwood, 2000), v.2, p. 904. Potter oath:

Letters received from Superintendents of Lights, Box 2, RG 26, National Archives.

21. Lighthouse notice: *Connecticut Gazette*, December 30, 1823.

22. Pleasonton instructions: Light-House Establishment, House Documents, Doc. 66, 24th Cong., 1st sess., p. 6. Stonington lighthouse account and log book, 1824-1828, Stonington Historical Society.

23. Keeper's report, January 1, 1831: custom house records, National Archives, Waltham.

24. Crawford to Pleasonton, May 24, 1831, Crawford correspondence, New London Maritime Society.

25. Crawford to Pleasonton, February 6, 1832, Crawford correspondence, New London Maritime Society. Crawford to Pleasonton, May 7, 1832, Crawford correspondence, New London Maritime Society. Crawford to William Potter, August 22, 1837, G.W. Blunt White Library, Mystic Seaport, VFM 184.

26. Communications from Messrs. E & G. Blunt, of New York, November 30, 1837, and February 22, 1838, Lighthouse Papers, pp. 94-106, 116-25.

27. Copy of the 2d Section of the Act of March 3, 1837, Lighthouse Papers, p. 36; and report of the Senate Committee on Commerce, March 22, 1838, Lighthouse Papers, pp. 125-33.

28. Report of Lieutenant George M. Bache, on Stonington: Lighthouse Papers, p. 211. On Bache's death, September 8, 1846: http://www/history.noaa.gov/hallofhonor/lineofduty.htm.

29. Bache report, pp. 211-212; Pleasonton reply to Bache, August 14, 1838, Lighthouse Papers, pp. 234-35.

30. Lester to Pleasonton, December 15, 1839, enclosing color drawing of seawall proposal by John Bishop; letters received from superintendents of lights, NC-31, Entry 17C, Record Group 26, National Archives; Pleasonton to Lester, March 10, 1840, Lighthouse Letters, vol. 15.

31. Pleasonton to Lester, April 22, 1840; Pleasonton to I.W.P. Lewis, April 23, 1840, Lighthouse Letters, 1839-1840, vol. 15, Entry 18, Record Group 26, National Archives.

32. Pleasonton to Lester, May 5, 1840, Lighthouse Letters, vol. 15, as cited above.

33. Pleasonton to Lester, June 4, 1840, Lighthouse Letters, vol. 15. See also the act of cession, granting the land to the United States, adopted by the Connecticut legislature on the same date, *Public Acts of the State of Connecticut, Passed May Session, 1840*, p. 29.

34. Stonington land records reveal a complex set of transactions involving the lighthouse lot. A year earlier, Crary and James Morris evidently obtained the land in a sale ordered by the New York Court of Chancery in foreclosure of a mortgage held by Crary against David Lord of New York City, who was the guardian of one Henry M. Bostwick, otherwise unidentified. Land Records, vol. 21, p. 394, May 2, 1839. The

Morris-Craig deed is listed at vol. 21, p. 37, May 18, 1840.

35. Text of contract: Lighthouse Deeds and Contracts, vol. 15, 1839-1847, Fifth Auditor's Office, Record Group 26, National Archives. Carving on stones visible in the seawall at Stonington Point today suggests previous use, but these markings are far from conclusive.

36. Text of contract, cited above.

37. Contracting practices: examination (dated April 8, 1842) of I.W.P. Lewis, Report of Evidence Relating to the Light-House Establishment, H.Doc. 183, 27th Cong., 3d Sess., September 8, 1842, pp. 6-20. Democrats: Lester was appointed by the Democratic Van Buren administration in 1838; Bishop claimed to be an active Democrat for fifty years: New London *Day*, "50 Years Ago," January 8, 1935.

38. Lester to Pleasonton, September 10, 1840; certification: signed statement by Richard Lester, March 26, 1842, both in letters from superintendents, as cited above.

39. Nomination of Huntington: Senate Journal, January 24, 1842; *Connecticut Gazette*, February 2, 1842. Brief biography: *A Genealogical Memoir of the Huntington Family in this Country* (1863), entry 1372.

40. Huntington to Pleasonton, March 25, 1842, letters from superintendents, as cited above. On the next day, the former collector, Lester, sent to Pleasonton his certification that the work on the Stonington lighthouse had been done satisfactorily.

41. Notice dated April 7, 1842, in New London *People's Advocate*, April 13, 1842.

42. Details of Potter family history prepared by Mary Beth Baker, from family records and U.S. Census returns.

43. Temporary appointment: Pleasonton to Huntington, May 14, 1842; permanent appointment: Pleasonton to Huntington, with enclosure, June 15, 1842, both in National Archives files, Waltham. Morgan Point keeper: Eliza Daboll was appointed in 1838, succeeding her husband; Mary Louise Clifford and J. Candace Clifford, *Women Who Kept the Lights* (Alexandria, Virginia: Cypress Communications, 2d ed., 2000) pp. 38-39.

44. Contract and drawings: labeled "With Mr. Huntington's July 5/42 Stonington Light House draft accompanying Charles H. Smith's contract of 13 May 42," records of the accounting officers of the Department of Treasury, civil contracts, contracts for the Lighthouse Service, 1800-1903, Box 001, Entry 153, Record Group 217, National Archives.

45. Huntington to Pleasonton, June 6, 1842; Smith and Brayton to Huntington, June 12, 1842, both in letters from superintendents, cited above.

46. Huntington to Pleasonton, dated June 14 [probably June 11], 1842, letters from superintendents, cited above.

47. Smith and Brayton to Huntington, June 12, 1842; G.R. Hallam to Huntington, June 15, 1842, both enclosed with Huntington to Pleasonton, June 15, 1842, in letters

from superintendents, cited above.

48. Receipt signed by Smith, July 2, 1842; Huntington to Pleasonton, August 29, 1842, both in letters from superintendents, cited above.

49. New London *People's Advocate*, May 15, 1843; *Genealogical Memoir of the Huntington Family*, entry 1372.

50. Pleasonton to Lester, May 17, 1843, Lighthouse Letters, cited above.

51. Examination of I.W.P. Lewis, April 8, 1842, cited above; W. Forward, secretary of the treasury, to Lewis, May 25, 1842, Lighthouse Papers (cited above) pp. 341-42.

52. "Ignorant and avaricious," Lewis report, January 31, 1843, in Lighthouse Papers, p. 341. Keepers: Lewis report, pp. 370-71.

53. Lester's reappointment was initially rejected by the Senate, but he was given a recess appointment and served until his death in 1846. See Senate Executive Journal, May 30, 1844; February 5, 1846.

54. Mussey appointment: Senate Executive Journal, February 5, 1846.

55. Mussey to Pleasonton, October 28, 1847, letters from superintendents of lighthouses, cited above; Pleasonton to Mussey, October 30, 1847, Lighthouse Letters, vol. 24.

56. "Filthy" references: Clifford and Clifford, *Women Who Kept the Lights*, pp. 40-41; Entremont, pp. 59-60.

57. Pleasonton to Mussey, October 4, 1848, Lighthouse Letters, as cited above.

58. Mussey to Pleasonton, October 10, 1848, letters from superintendents, cited above. Captain Howland: Francis Ross Holland, *America's Lighthouses: An Illustrated History* (1981), p. 31.

59. Report of the general superintendent of the light-house establishment, 31st Cong., 2d, Sess., December 14, 1850.

60. Dyer Potter to Pleasonton, December 5, 1849, Lighthouse Letters, cited above. Dyer's death: Potter family records, compiled by Mary Beth Baker.

61. End of era: documents relating to the creation and first report of the Lighthouse Board, in Lighthouse Papers, pp. 550-724. Winslow Lewis death: *Boston Evening Transcript*, May 20, 1850. Pleasonton death: *Daily National Intelligencer*, Washington, February 2, 1855; obituary in *Philadelphia Inquirer*, February 3, 1855. I. W. P. Lewis death: See Robert Fraser, "I. W. P. Lewis: Father of America's Lighthouse System," *The Keeper's Log*, Winter 1989, pp. 8-10. Note: I.W.P. Lewis's name (Isaac William Penn Lewis) was often mistranscribed as "J.W.P Lewis."

62. Potter-Barker family data by Mary Beth Baker, as cited above.

63. Luther Ripley: basic biographical research by Mary Beth Baker. See *A Memorial Volume of the Bi-Centennial Celebration of the Town of Windham* (Hartford, 1893). War of 1812: U.S., War of 1812 Service Records, 1812-1815, National Archives, microfilm roll box 175, roll 602. Political activity: see 1832-33 editions of *Samuel*

Green's Connecticut Annual Register; Hartford American Mercury, February 21, 1831; *Hartford Times*, April 8, 1833; October 27, 1838.

64.   Date of appointment as inspector estimated from letter from B. Pomeroy, Stonington collector, to C. W. Rockwell, commissioner of customs, May 12, 1849, annual report of the Secretary of the Treasury, 1851. Removal from office: *New London Morning News,* November 14, 1845. Hamlin remonstrance: Senate Journal, January 24, 1850. No occupation: 1850 United States Census, National Archives microfilm publication M432, roll 48.

65.   Appointment as keeper: *Washington Evening Star,* April 20, 1854; Register of Officers and Agents, Civil, Military, and Naval in the Service of the United States as of September 30, 1854, p. 30. Family: 1850, 1860 United States Census. Luther Ripley, Jr., listed in the 1850 census as a sailor, both at home and on a sailing vessel, is not listed in 1860. Luther Ripley's wives died in 1828, 1834, and 1851.

66.   New lens: Report on the Finances, Senate Documents, 1857, p. 598. On the superiority of the Fresnel lens, see the report by Lieutenants Thornton A. Jenkins and Richard Bache, June 22, 1846, Lighthouse Papers, pp. 448-65.

67.   Resignation: Record of Lights—Keepers' Names . . . National Archives microfilm. "Secesh": William Augustus Croffut and John Moses Morris, *The Military and Civil History of Connecticut during the War of 1861-65* (1868), p. 105; *Boston Evening Transcript*, August 14, 1861.

68.   Ripley's retirement: U.S. Census for 1870; *Queens County Sentinel*, August 31, 1870. Death, March 19, 1878, Find a Grave online program, Chaplin Center Cemetery.

69.   Winthop Hand: roster of Stonington lighthouse keepers, National Archives microfilm.

70.   Burgess: murder witness: *Norwich Aurora*, January 23, 1867; *Mystic Pioneer*, February 2, 1867. Biographical information from the 1880 federal census and the 1881 *Stonington Directory*. Obituary: *Hartford Courant*, February 5, 1894.

71.   Noyes: federal census returns, 1870 and 1880; Stonington Directory, 1881; *New Haven Register,* February 27, 1899; New London *Day*, June 18, 1909, noting Noyes's transfer from Latimer Reef to Ram Island lightship, his last position.

72.   Benjamin F. Pendleton was linked to the family of the first keeper; he was a brother-in-law of Amelia Barker Sheffield, a granddaughter of William and Patty Potter. See federal census returns, 1870 and 1880, and the Pendleton genealogy in Richard Anson Wheeler, *History of the Town of Stonington* (New London, 1900), pp. 531-36. See also obituary in the *Westerly Sun*, February 18, 1909, the day of his death. Frederick Starr Pendleton: letter to authors from Arthur M. Delmhorst, February 13, 2013; obituary in *New York Times*, August 27, 1951. Note also an oral history interview with Frank Pendleton, a grandson of Benjamin Franklin Pendleton, June

1973; the interviewer is George L. Campbell, and the recording is in the Society's Woolworth Library.

72. Annual Report of the Chief of Engineers, 1875, Part 2, vol. 2, pp. 239-42.

73. Annual Report, 1875, pp. 242-48; Annual Report of the Chief of Engineers, 1884, Part 1, p. 632.

74. Report of the Lighthouse Board, 1886, p. 13; Report of the Lighthouse Board, 1888, p. 54.

75. Closing: Lighthouse Board, Notice to Mariners No. 60 of 1889, October 12, 1889, National Archives.

76. Breakwater Light: inspection report, Stonington Breakwater Light Station, December 19, 1889, United States Lighthouse Society, www.uslhs/national archives/Stoningtonfiles/lh_access.htm.

77. Samuel D. Pendleton: *Official Register of the United States*, 1889, p. 302; New London *Day*, December 17, 1898.

78. Beckwith: Short biography in *Biographical Review, containing Life Sketches of Leading Citizens of New London County, Connecticut*, vol. 26 (1898), 421-22; stories in the New London *Day*, December 10, 1898; January 18 and February 11, 1899; and in the *New Haven Register*, February 13, 1899. Staplin and gun emplacement: *Providence Journal*, April 28, 1898.

79. Fuller: *Master of Desolation: The Reminiscences of Capt. Joseph J. Fuller*, edited by Briton Cooper Busch (Mystic, 1980). See Busch's introduction, pp. xiii-xxv; and list of voyages, pp. 288-89. Transfer to Lighthouse Board: Report of the Corps of Engineers, 1901, p. 177.

80. Stranded: New London *Day*, January 9, 1908; breakwater light: *Day*, March 31, 1911; launch: *Day*, April 25, 1912; Scouts: *Day*, January 8, 1916. Fuller's retirement and death: *Master of Desolation*, p. xviii.

81. "Keeper's Dwelling at Stonington Breakwater, Connecticut," Senate Report 131, 59th Cong., 1st Sess., January 11, 1906, incorporating letter of December 7, 1901, from the Department of the Treasury. *Stonington Mirror*, June 3, 1908.

82. Louis Poutray: federal census, 1920; oral history interview of Eleanor Poutray Mudge, September 5, 1994, interviewer unidentified, cassette tape recording in Woolworth Library.

83. Stonington Historical and Genealogical Society history: Taliaferro Boatwright, "History of the Stonington Historical Society," *Historical Footnotes*, vol. 32 (May 1995). *Stonington Mirror*. August 27, 1909.

84. The flag's history is summarized in Susan J. Jerome, "The Stonington Battle Flag," *Connecticut Explored*, v. 10 (Summer 2012).

85. "Historical objects": *The Stonington Battle Centennial* (Stonington, 1915), p. 13. G.R. Putnam to Henry R. Palmer, July 7, 1913; J. T. Yates to Palmer, July 29, 1913,

in Society records all held in Woolworth Library. New London *Day*, July 16, 1913.

86. Minutes, meeting of November 5, 1913, Society records. New London *Day*, January 8, February 3, 1914.

87. Society exhibition: *Stonington Battle Centennial*, pp. 61-62. Sheffield: Potter family data, compiled by Mary Beth Baker.

88. Success: *Stonington Battle Centennial*, p. 62.

89. "Recently useless": Palmer to J. Culbert Palmer, August 4, 1924, Society records; SPNEA contact: Wm. Sumner Appleton to Williams, March 9, 1917.

90. H.B. Bowerman to Williams, April 25, 1924.

91. J. S. Conway to Williams, May 2, 1924; Williams to Conway, October 16, 1924; Conway to Williams, October 26, 1924.

92. Henry R. Palmer to J. Culbert Palmer, August 4, 1924; J. Culbert Palmer to Henry R. Palmer, August 6, 1924; minutes, annual meeting, August __, 1924, in Society records.

93. Minutes, meeting of December 29, 1924; "Historical Society Appeal for Endowment," undated, both in Society records.

94. Anne Atwood Dodge to Williams, February 7, 1925, in Society records.

95. Conway to Williams, April 17, 1925; Williams to Superintendent of Lighthouses, May 12, 1925; G.R. Putnam, Commissioner, to Freeman, May 12, 1925, in Society records.

96. Conway to Freeman, May 23, 1925; Simmons to Culbert Palmer, May 19, 1925, in Society records.

97. Deed: United States to Eugene Atwood, June 8, 1925, vol. 65, p, 276, Stonington land records.

98. Minutes, meeting of July 17, 1925, Society records.

99. Annual meeting, September 25, 1925; delivery of check and deed: Atwood's secretary to Williams, October 24, 1925, both in Society records. The deed is recorded on September 26, 1925, vol. 65, p. 298, in Stonington land records. Atwood obituary: *New York Times*, June 4, 1926.

100. Drawing of October 25, 1925, in Society records.

101. Darrell obituary, New London *Day*, August 9, 1989.

102. Karin Peterson, "From Stone House to Glass House: Connecticut's House Museums," offers a brief summary: http://www.cttrust.org/index.cgi/11915.

103. Laura E. Richards, *Captain January* (Boston, 1890).

104. Lighthouse Board, *Instructions to Light-House Keepers*, 1881, p. 6.

105. Minutes, board of governors, December 26, 1925, Society records.

106. On density of Portuguese (Azorean) families in the south Borough, see census tables reprinted in Henrietta M. Mayer, *South of the Cannons: The Portuguese Families of Stonington, Connecticut* (Stonington, 1978, 2011). Minutes, December 26, 1925.

107. Minutes, officers and committee heads, July 28, 1926; minutes, board of governors, August 20, 1926, in Society records.

108. "Scheme A," plan by York & Sawyer, New York, undated, in Society records. Inspection: Mary Beth Baker, account of walking inspection by Stephen C. Marshall, August 20, 2010, in Society records.

109. Invoices and receipts in Society records.

110. York to Williams, November 27, 1928; minutes, special meeting, April 13, 1929, Society records.

111. United States deed to Eugene Atwood, September 26, 1925, as cited above. Weather tower: acting secretary of agriculture to secretary of commerce, August 3, 1917, copy in Society records; New London *Day*, November 21, 1917. J. Culbert Palmer to Bureau of Lighthouses, June 28, 1926; Palmer to Richard Freeman, June 28, 1926; J.C. Conway to Palmer, July 12, 1926, Society records.

112. Removal of breakwater lighthouse: See Coast Guard tabulation at www.uscg.mil/weblighthouses/lcht.asp. Conway to Richard Freeman, July 15, 1926; Department of Commerce, Lighthouse Service, "Form of Proposal for Sale of Stonington Harbor Light Station Reservation," August 3, 1926; minutes, meeting of July 18, 1935, copies in Society records.

113. Deed, United States to Wilson Fitch Smith, September 27, 1926, vol. 65, p. 464, Stonington land records. Current information on house at 5 Water Street, Stonington, summarized, e.g., at www.trulia.com.

114. Minutes, June 25, 1927, Society records.

115. Register of attendance, August 10, 1927. Lighthouse accounts in Society records.

116. Joseph Santos: George L. Campbell in *Historical Footnotes*, vol. 16 (February 1979); obituary: New London *Day*, March 1, 1979.·

117. Deed, United States to Borough of Stonington, December 22, 1932, Stonington land records, vol. 71, pp. 280-81.

118. Tearoom information is in Society records.

119. Minutes of meetings, Society records.

120. *Connecticut, A Guide to Its Roads, Lore, and People*" (Boston, 1938), p. 303.

121. Minutes, 1938-1939; treasurer's report, 1939, in Society records.

122. "Guy Penè du Bois, Artist in Residence," *Historical Footnotes*, vol. 43 (November 2006). Painting: "Portia LeBrun in a Pink Blouse," 1942.

123. Register of visitors, July 17, 1946; minutes, May 9, 1947, June 8, 1948, in Society records.

124. Coale's paintings are discussed at http://www.history.navy.mil/ac/artist/c/coale/coale1.htm.

125. Hurlbuts: interview with their daughter, Elsa Hurlbut Cole, August 2, 2012.

126. Stephen Hurlbut, President's Report to Annual Meeting, February 5, 1958,

Historical Society records; Hurlbut, report to December 1948, meeting.

127. Hurlbut report, 1958; interview with Elsa Cole.

128. Minutes, meeting of March 8, 1949. Flag restoration: Betsy Wade, "A New Chapter for the 1814 Battle Flag," and related material in *Historical Footnotes*, vol. 41 (February 2004).

129. Griffith Baily Coale funeral in Stonington, New London *Day*, August 24, 1950. Hurlbuts' report, annual meeting, 1950; Hurlbut report, 1958.

130. The Hurlbut plaque is displayed above a door in the Old Lighthouse Museum.

131. Bank and plans: Taliaferro Boatwright, "The Stonington Historical Society," *Historical Footnotes*, vol. 32 (May 1995).

132. Arcade: New London *Day*. October 15, 1951; Mary Beth Baker, "The Arcade: Last of an Endangered Species?" *Historical Footnotes*, vol. 44 (August 2007). Bank: New London *Day*, April 7, 1950. Huxtable: *On Architecture: Collected Reflections on a Century of Change* (New York, 2008): "The serendipitous reuse that continually regenerates historic stock is the only kind of preservation that works" (p. 352).

133. Whitehall: New London *Day*, March 31, 1993; Stonington Historical Society, *Whitehall and Its Restoration* (Stonington, 1970). On sale of Whitehall, see report by the Society's president, Dr. Norman H. Boas, *Historical Footnotes*, vol. 31 (February 1994).

134. Powel's work: George L. Campbell, "The Lighthouse Museum Collections," *Historical Footnotes*, vol. 32 (August 1995).

135. Mary Beth Baker, "Historical Liaisons: Part II," *Historical Footnotes*, vol. 47 (February 2010).

136. Campbell, "The Lighthouse Museum Collections."

137. See relevant reports in the Old Lighthouse Museum column in *Historical Footnotes*

138. Louise Pittaway interview, cited above.

139. D'Entremont, "Louise Pittaway: Keeper of Stonington's Lighthouse and Legacy," *Lighthouse Digest*, May 2004.

140. See relevant issues of *Historical Footnotes*.

141. Bruce Clouette, nomination form, National Register Historic Places, July 8, 1975.

The text of this book was set in Adobe Caslon and printed by McNaughton & Gunn in Saline, Michigan.